CHOYO WILSON-DANIEL

rich ON PURPOSE

THE INSPIRED WOMAN'S GUIDE TO
MONEY + LIFE + SELF LOVE

Published by
Hasmark Publishing
www.hasmarkpublishing.com

Copyright ©2019 Choyo Wilson-Daniel
First Edition

Permission should be addressed in writing to Choyo Wilson-Daniel at Choyow1@gmail.com

Editor: Corinne Casazza
corinnecasazza@gmail.com

Cover & Book Design: Anne Karklins
anne@hasmarkpublishing.com

ISBN 13: 978-1-989161-93-7

ISBN 10: 1989161936

Hasmark
PUBLISHING

To my beautiful daughters Hannah and Olivia –
being your mother has been the ultimate gift.
Every day I spend with you, watching you grow into the
fierce women you'll become, makes me feel like I am
the richest person in the Universe.

To my loving and supportive Husband, Charles.
Your strength, wisdom and unwavering support is unlike any other.
With your love, I can accomplish anything.

Acknowledgements

Writing this book was a complete labor of love, a test of strength and life lessons. I relied on the wisdom and support of so many of you – friends and family that have encouraged and challenged me to grow all these years – I love you. You inspire me every day.

I want to especially acknowledge my mentors Bob Proctor, Kendall Summerhawk, and Peggy McColl – you guys are the best to ever do it!

And to my mother, Barbara James-Norman, for giving me the original blueprint to living life as a confident, ambitious and compassionate woman – if I can be nearly half as good as you, I would be ok. I love you.

TABLE OF CONTENTS

CHAPTER ONE

MIND ON MY MONEY AND MY MONEY ON MY MIND

I know you've read the books. I know you've listened to the tapes, watched the videos and heck, you probably have a few daily affirmations you repeat to yourself: "I am wealthy. I am confident. I am strong." And while all of these things are so very important to do, they are not working.

Why is that?

Am I not doing this right?

You're still in a standstill. Or repeating the same tired cycle. What's going on?

Girl, I know. This was me. Was. And no, I didn't win the lottery, marry rich, invest in Google in its early stages, inherit a nest egg from Great Aunt Dottie or uncover a secret pre-Civil War heirloom in my attic. Nope. It wasn't real estate, nor a massive promotion at work that changed the game for me. **It was my inner work.** I had to almost lose my first home to foreclosure. Luckily, I didn't have to go through that process, but my name being on the list was enough to wake me up. It was then I realized that I needed to do something different. I had to do a complete upgrade on my mind. I had to re-evaluate my belief system. The process was so interesting and scary! You can only imagine my reaction when I finally realized that I was operating from a belief system that wasn't established by me, rather It was passed down from at least four generations.

Let me explain.

Mindset? Say What?

As a child, I always wanted to help people. I mean *always*. I was a really sensitive child. Today, they would call me an Empath – but all I knew was that I felt other people's emotions.

Aside from being a sensitive child, I had big dreams. Or, more specifically, I always dreamed of being rich. I felt like money would solve a lot of problems in the world. Where did this come from? Well, I witnessed families split because of money, friendships ended because of money. Women going to prison because they were doing every last thing they could to earn money to raise their families.

And then there was my direct environment. My step father was an entrepreneur. I saw the money coming in. I knew that I wanted to be like him. It appeared as if he was helping a lot of people. And I wanted that. For me it wasn't a dream of marrying a rich man (although there is absolutely nothing wrong with that). I dreamed of being an entrepreneur. I didn't fully flesh out that plan (and my parents never talked about the ups and downs and cycles of business) but I knew I'd get there. I just had to:

1. Wear trendy, designer clothes (you know to be successful and for people to believe you're successful, you need to look successful)

2. Drive a cute, small, but foreign luxury car (see absurd rationale above)

3. Go to college. Graduate college. At the top of my class. Early.

4. Keep the Faith and seek the kingdom of God

5. Have an A+ credit rating of 850

6. Start a business of something (trust me, I have no shortage of ideas) that easily produces $25K a month

7. Pay my tithes

That's it. That's my plan. Or that was my plan. And while I was steadily trying to work this plan, I was internally fighting with myself because I thought *something about my thinking isn't aligning with some of my beliefs*. It just didn't make sense. My environment and my mindset didn't support my materialistic point of view. But I knew in my heart of hearts that this was the way. The only way.

There are sooo many things wrong with this plan. Starting with the fact that it isn't a plan at all. It's a mindset.

Do you know what I mean by mindset? Simply put, a mindset is the overriding beliefs you hold about something which impacts our overall thoughts about it. It drives how you make decisions every day. Your mindset has a HUGE impact on your ability to achieve your goals. An easy way to remember why your mindset is so influential is:

Beliefs → Thoughts → Actions

So, while I had this (ahem) stellar plan, my thoughts about my plan were not on point. Where did I get those thoughts? My beliefs surrounding money were programmed in me from a very young age. From my parents and my experiences. Those things were deeply planted in my head – so much so, that they're automatic – I didn't even question them. I was taught to get a higher education, pay my tithes and… I saw my mother and step-father go through cycles of feast or famine. The impact of money on my household always operated in extremes.

Talk about a mixed message. They'd have injections of money, then they'd be broke. My stepfather, who was a businessman, would close a deal and money would pour in. Unfortunately, operating like that means money is short lived. When I was a young, impressionable girl with big goals, my parents never talked about the ups and downs of running a business or how it worked, so I had no idea.

On the other hand, my mother had a very strong faith. She taught me to always believe God will make a way. Whatever you want, God will grant it. However, my mother never really talked about the other side of our reality; when the business deals didn't go through. Avoiding these hard conversations ultimately taught me a lesson that she probably never intended: how to deal with rejection (with an unhealthy coping method). She had pumped me up so much. I didn't even think rejection was an option, but in the real world it happens all the time. It was almost like some teachings I'd had. They taught me to fantasize and believe the impossible, but not the other side of the spectrum. Even though I had seen the other side. It just wasn't talked about.

Again, more mixed messages! My belief system started off a little something like this:

1. Money is awesome if you have it, but it sucks when you don't

2. If you're still crazy enough to try to get Rich, don't forget to take all of us with you or you suck!

3. Money always runs out

4. Money doesn't grow on trees

Seriously, I believed all of this. My parents were very creative and found ways to bring income in the home. I certainly inherited this trait. But when it came time to set out on my own, plan in hand, it didn't feel right. I felt conflicted. I couldn't get it right. I never had a problem earning money. I had a problem keeping money.

This clearly was a money block. A money block is anything that blocks you around earning, attracting, receiving, having, keeping, saving, managing and leveraging the money you want. I know this now, but I didn't fully grasp it then.

And of course, I didn't know I was conflicted. I just knew what I planned to do and got incredibly frustrated when I started living the life of feast and famine. I was not accomplishing my goals.

Here's the clincher – do you want to know what 'not accomplishing anything' looked like for me? Well, let me tell you:

1. A Bachelor's and two Master's degrees

2. A professional licensure as a clinical therapist

3. A homeowner by the age 25

4. A luxury car

5. Married to a Pastor

Pretty cool, right? I'd say so. But I also had started multiple ventures that fizzled out in the middle of the process. I was living paycheck to paycheck.

In between these cycles of feast and famine I was church-going and hustling. Every time I failed I thought *There's never enough resources – time, money, smarts, you name it.*

What followed thought patterns? Pending foreclosure. Lay-offs. Brink of shame. Guilt. Robbing Pete to pay Paul. For years.

WAIT, POVERTY IS A MINDSET?

Before you get all politically correct me, let me explain. I am keenly aware that there are millions of people who live in poverty who are not making the choice to be there. I am keenly aware of the systemic social, economic and political forces that influence and, essentially, trap people in poverty. Over 80% of the world lives on less than $10 per day. If you're reading this book, have running water in your house and are able to have at least one meal today, then you are extremely wealthy. **We all are.**

That's not what I'm talking about. I'm talking about a mindset I carried that was dictated by my inner (subconscious) beliefs. Think of a poverty mindset as unconsciously sabotaging yourself from flowing into the energy of abundance. When you frame it in that mindset, it manifests in your life in many ways, including:

1. Never being able to save money or make more than you need
2. Always being watchful/envious of what other people have
3. Thinking that happiness is a destination and not a journey (I'll be happy when I have the house, or the car etc.)
4. Being afraid to spend money or spending most of your money the minute it hits your checking account.
5. Living paycheck to paycheck.

Or you say (or think) things like:

6. I work so hard and I still can't make ends meet
7. I'll never be able to afford a vacation
8. I'll take what I can get for this project, even if it's giving away my services for free

And so on...

Let me tell you, a poverty mindset is so very destructive because it puts us in the role of helpless victim. It convinces us that our narrative is set in stone and we have no control over what happens to us; no control of our destiny. Life is full of suffering, yet somehow easier, when we believe everything that happens to us is the result of outside forces. With a poverty mindset, **you're always focusing on never having enough**.

Astonishing, right? **But, if you recognize some of these characteristics in you, don't immediately default to shame and guilt**. In all my years in the Church, as a congregation member and a member of leadership, I see this among Christians (myself included) all the time. Think about it – the Bible commands us to be diligent and wise, and promises that those traits inevitably lead to a prosperous life. The opposite of diligence and wisdom is folly and the life of the sluggard. If you think God has good things to say about the foolish, you might want to reread the Book of Proverbs. Instead of embracing the principles of Proverbs –hard work, discipline, sowing and reaping – we embrace the poverty mindset, which says, "The mess I'm in isn't my fault, so I'm powerless to change it. I'll just sit here watching Netflix, scrolling the 'gram and keekeeing with my girls. God is in control, so I'm sure He'll figure everything out eventually and make my life better."

Or we think that being poor is noble and brings you closer to God. But neither of these thoughts don't really mesh well with what God wants for our life, the real world or what you really desire, do they? God has given you the beautiful gift of agency, imagination and intelligence – what do you think needs to happen?

ABUNDANCE AS A MINDSET

As you may have guessed, an abundance mindset is very much the opposite of a scarcity or poverty mindset. An abundance mindset keeps in mind every possible, favorable outcome for your financial situation while allowing you to be open to each one.

"The abundance mentality… is the paradigm that there is plenty out there and enough to spare for everybody. It results in sharing of prestige, of recognition, of profits, of decision making. It opens possibilities, options, alternatives, and creativity."
– The Seven Habits of Highly Effective People, **Stephen Covey**

We've ultimately got two choices in life, **move in fear or move in love.** Scarcity and abundance are extensions of that same ethos – we can choose between viewing the world as abundant or limited in terms of relationships, wealth and resources.

Thinking to yourself there just isn't enough time, money, love or whatever, or having an "if only" mindset (i.e., if only I got that dream job, paycheck, vacation etc., then I could be happy) drives how we set up our businesses, interact with our colleagues, run our lives and teach our children. **We feel threatened by other people's success.** When we operate out of fear/scarcity – we react and act hastily, shrinking deadlines and our imaginations, asking for the impossible and giving ourselves no options.

Since we're on the subject of abundance, please know that *Your* abundance in no way takes away from someone else's. **You and I have been trained to make an agreement with Lack, and the retraining of our thinking is to remove our agreement with Lack.** You must begin to agree with the nature of Abundance and that is a retraining process in itself. **What we are seeking to have, we must be of. Whatever you pray for, believe you should have it.**

For example, when I work with my clients, I hear all the time, "I want to make a million dollars."

As a therapist, I'm not only trained to listen for what is being said, but what isn't being said. When I hear this desire from my clients, it usually sounds more like a dirty confession than a proud assertion.

I usually work with clients on their money blocks and on acknowledging and breaking their Agreement with Lack. I tell them wanting more money is natural. There's nothing shameful about wanting a better life. Having a limited income inhibits your choices, freedom and quality of life. It also prevents you from being able to make a meaningful impact on the lives of others.

If you happen to make more and you're committed to the chains of fear and guilt, you'll forever repeat the feast/famine cycle. So, let's let go of any guilt, shame or feelings of unworthiness and get on with changing your programming.

You create abundance from the inside out. And you do that by changing what you focus on. There is enough for YOU, and there is enough for everyone. The question is...

Do you believe you are an abundant being?

As above, so below.

As within, so without.

Vibrate to a higher state of thinking and feeling. The state of vibration of your body makes you act in a certain way which produces your results.

THOUGHTS

FEELING

VIBRATION

ACTIONS

RESULTS

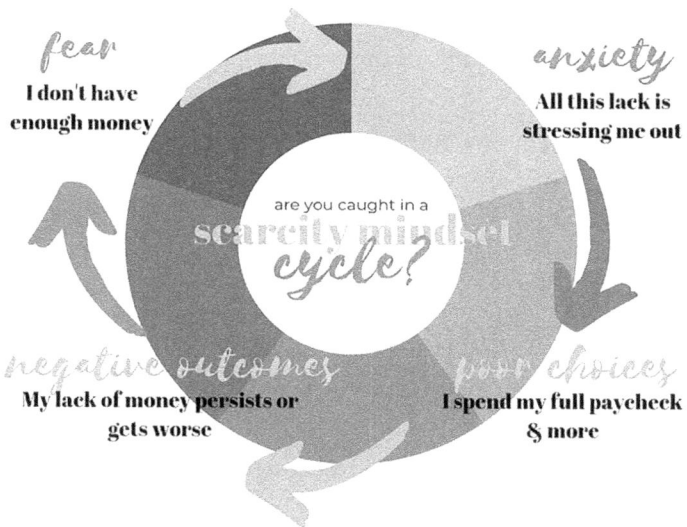

fear
I don't have
enough money

anxiety
All this lack is
stressing me out

are you caught in a
scarcity mindset
cycle?

negative outcomes
My lack of money persists or
gets worse

poor choices
I spend my full paycheck
& more

The mental awareness of prosperity always precedes wealth in your material world. That's why it's so important to employ your faith. Faith is the ability to see the invisible and believe in the incredible, and that is what enables believers to receive what the masses think is impossible. We must learn not to look at the visible supply. For example: Looking at your low bank account balance...

BUT you've gotta eat, breathe, sleep, think and, most importantly, *believe* abundance.

Start with what you can be thankful for, and get your mind into that vibration. Then watch the good that starts to come, because one good thought leads to another and before you know it, you've got some abundance momentum going.

I know, I know. It sounds airy fairy. But it's not. It's science. Psychologists note that when we meet our expectations of abundance – more money, time, and resources; we quickly return to the same level of happiness we had prior to gaining our abundance. If we're unhappy now and we achieve more, it's still not enough. How do we overcome that overwhelming notion? The very same psychologists recommend that reminding yourself of all you have and recognizing that more will never fill you up, allows you to see just how privileged you are. **It's a very deliberate re-focusing of the word *enough*: you being enough, you having enough, you accomplishing enough.** It's about you practicing Gratitude. And you might have guessed it by now – Science backs this up! Being grateful triggers dopamine in your brain, that feel-good neurotransmitter, that allows you to feel happier, healthier and have a more expansive, abundant mindset.

DIAGNOSING THE HEALTH OF YOUR MONEY RELATIONSHIP

Let's look at your relationship with money from a different perspective. We've been getting all in our feelings and talking about your emotions and beliefs about money, but just for fun, let's put yourself on the other side of the table.

By that I mean, let's imagine money to be your mate, partner, spouse, husband, Bae, anything you want to call it, and see what it would say about its relationship with you. This is a fun exercise. I want you to imagine money writing a letter to you that would address the following:

- How would money describe your history with it over the course of your lifetime?
- What period of your life did you have the best relationship with money and why?
- Does money feel that you are ready and willing to receive it? Why or why not?
- What belief do you say you have about money, but fail to act on?
- Does money think you believe you have a financial ceiling? If so, what amount/limit would money say you've placed on it?
- What would money ask you to do differently to improve your relationship with it?

I promise you, it will be worth every minute you spend into raising your awareness of how you think, what you believe and how you behave when it comes to money. It will help you develop a more abundant mindset.

This exercise switches the focus of what you've accomplished in life (results) and puts you in the flow of abundance – which is appreciation, gratitude, forgiveness, compassion – just mindfulness in general! Like… actually appreciating and not taking anything for granted. Let's begin with some simple ways you can start applying an abundance mindset in your real life.

Abundance Mindset #1: I Am Thankful for My Paychecks

Embrace the wealth you already have. No matter how little you feel you have today, if you have the means to purchase and read this book, you have more than you think. Be grateful (remember the dopamine!).

Abundance Mindset #2: I Am Thankful for This Moment

By shifting from the fear of not having enough time, to gratitude for the time you have, your mind becomes more relaxed and can focus on the task at hand. You do the job well and feel good about completing something to the best of your ability. If the task includes another person, then sharing quality time with that person instead of juggling e-mails and texts will result in a stronger relationship. (Read: multi-tasking is a gratitude killer).

Abundance Mindset #3: I Am Thankful for Money

Say this out loud: "I am so thankful that money flows into my life freely." See how this simple statement is a much more positive way to look at money in general? It's okay to be thankful for money! When we uncover your money blocks (don't worry, I'll give you a few exercises to help you understand which ones are yours soon), you'll most likely uncover where your conflict is and how to solve it.

"Gratitude is the muscle that makes miracles happen."

Abundance Mindset #4: Self-compassion

Being human means that you're still going to experience life's ups and downs, but when you adopt an abundant mindset, you become more resilient. Abundance and resilience go hand-in-hand. Resilience requires forgiveness and compassion. Compassion for others, but most importantly, yourself. Remember, you can only have as much compassion for someone else as you have for yourself.

Let's change this.

Resilience is the ability to self-soothe — a process that has three steps or phases. (More science proof for you). Is resilience something some folks are born with and others have to develop? Well, some may have a more natural proclivity to exercising resilience, but it can be developed by anyone. According to Psychology professor Kristin Neff, there is a three-step framework to developing resilience.

1. First, admit an experience or situation is painful, that you're suffering, you're struggling. Maybe you're burnt out, things aren't going the way you want, or you just received some bad news. Feel the discomfort in the moment, and don't try to hide from it or dismiss it. According to Neff, simply labeling an emotion starts to calm you down.

2. Second, acknowledge this type of pain is a shared human experience. Life is full of terrible, trying, maddening, sorrowful situations. It happens to the best of us, and none of us is alone. There are no new stresses right now. Someone else on this planet has or will experience what you're feeling. We selfishly isolate when we are going through things, but reconnecting is key to resilience.

3. Third, figure out what kind, mindful action you can take to feel better right now. What can you give yourself to get even just a little relief? Maybe it's getting out of the room, or choosing to sleep or exercise over work, or admitting you don't know the answer. Play with your pet. Do something kind for yourself – that means nourishing, grounding,

something that makes you feel concretely better after you do it. Neff says even putting your hand over your heart for a minute can get oxytocin (the "feel-good" hormone) flowing to provide emotional relief.

Additionally, studies have shown that self-compassion is correlated with much greater grit. Quickly running through these three steps is one way to maintain an abundant mindset in the most stressful or emotional situations. Everyone is bound to run into scarcity, but by taking a few self-compassion breaks during the day, you gain a tremendous amount of emotional flexibility and resilience.

Abundance Mindset #5: Generosity

Know your personal currency. What is your value and how can you offer value to the people around you? Research shows the most powerful and happy people are at the center of large networks constantly giving to their connections. Too many people feel like they have nothing to offer when they have a ton: attention, presence, kindness, knowledge, access to resources. The abundant mindset sees opportunities to appreciate others, and the result is more abundance. The best form of appreciation is precision – knowing specifically what you can and will contribute. It recognizes something specific and the impact it made.

Remember, you're not here to just get by. You're not here to earn just enough to pay your mortgage or your car. You're here to serve and be the best you can be.

Few people ever grasp the simple truth that all we need to do to improve our results is to think big, dream big and envision a larger, more prosperous idea into the infinite current of life. Instead, most of us strangle our supply with energy-impoverished thoughts of doubt and fear, which entirely cut off the inflow of prosperity. And it keeps us mediocre. At its best, it keeps us looking good for the 'gram.

But you must understand you already have in substance, if not in physical form, you have everything necessary to produce prosperity in your material world. The determining factors for you to attain the results you want are **desire** and **expectation**. In other words, use desire to change your money story, and you'll get different results.

I'll give you an example: do you remember when I told you that I was always entrepreneurial at heart? Well, I would think that every time one of my ventures failed was because I did not have all of the resources available to me that other successful entrepreneurs did; meaning money, working 18 hours days, access to the right networks, blah blah blah. But after many false starts and failures, I learned to redefine what I thought determined success, and understand that some of my money blocks were "it takes money to make money" and "making money is hard." False and false. I kept stalling and failing because these money blocks were not aligned with my hustle. I didn't see that I was surrounded by many folks who could easily be my mentors, that I had money that I could have tapped into via my 401K to jumpstart my venture, and that I was only one degree removed from powerful connections that my friends and family could have made. It wasn't until I removed these blocks that I was able to see all the talents I possessed and the resources that I had to accomplish my goals. And the rest was history.

CTRL ALT DEL YOUR WAY TO A NEW MONEY STORY

Are you ready to go deep and uncover some of your money blocks, limiting beliefs, emotional wounds and money stories so you can be aware of the sneaky beliefs that are holding you back? Good. It's time to get to work.

We've all got a story. Remember the saying "knowing is half the battle?" Well, knowing your money story will help change the trajectory of your life... trust me.

Understanding your money story is about becoming intimately aware of the thought processes and belief patterns that are driving your behavior when it comes to money (the lack of money or abundance of money). It's time to get rid of the unhelpful stories running the show and bringing you the same broken down results in your financial life.

Like I mentioned earlier, you're going to have to put in the work to change your results. But it's good work, I promise. And I've developed an easy-to-remember process on how you can begin to consciously be the boss of you!

It's called Control, Alternate and Delete. Or, CTRL, ALT, DEL. Just like the computer keys that handle ANY task.

Once we take **CONTROL** of our focus, and then **ALTER** our beliefs to healthier ones that serve us (by choosing a new, empowering story), we get to **DELETE** the old ways of thinking and behaving that create resistance to getting the results we really want!

Rest assured, my approach is rooted in science. It all has to do with neural pathways and the concept of neuroplasticity.

Neural pathways are like superhighways of nerve cells that transmit messages. As you travel over the superhighway many times, and the pathway becomes more and more solid. So, for example, as you may go to a specific food or cigarettes or alcohol or shopping (the list is endless) for comfort over and over, and that forms a brain pathway. But here is the hopeful part (and the basis for CTRL ALT DEL) the brain is always changing and you can forge new pathways and create new habits (neuroplasticity).

For example, instead of thinking, "I have to work harder to make more money," and feeling stressed and overwhelmed, we choose the thought, "It's easy for me to make money" and commit to that thought – forming new behavior patterns based on this new thinking. THAT's money mindset at work right there!

Let's apply this principle in real life. We'll use this process with your money story. Grab a journal or anything you'd like to write in.

STEP 1:

Think back on your relationship with money throughout your life. Write down what comes to mind – any words, phrases, emotions or events that stand out in your mind when you reflect on each of these topics:

- Your experience of money as a young child
- Your experience of money as a teenager
- Your experience of money as an adult in your 20s
- Your experience of money as an adult in your 30s
- Your experience of money as an adult in your 40s…50s….60s… all stages of your life
- Your mother's relationship with money
- Your father's relationship with money
- Any standout memories of money (good and bad)

STEP 2:

Girl, don't be afraid – this is your AHA moment! Take a look through all the ideas and perspectives you've uncovered and notice any patterns that stand out. Think about how these thoughts or beliefs have been showing up in your financial life. How do your current actions or results connect to these beliefs?

List any patterns, insights or realizations. Aha!

Awareness is SO POWERFUL. You've already entered a new phase in your life. Take a moment to acknowledge and appreciate yourself for doing this work. Going through past memories can be challenging, but it's so, so worth it when you gain that insight to change your life moving forward.

STEP 3:

More good work ahead! Now take all the beliefs, emotions, insights and patterns you've identified and cross them out. Next to them, write a new, empowering, abundance statement or story to replace the old scarcity one. Take baby steps and only write beliefs that actually feel believable to you.

For example, if you're ready to drop your parent's favorite saying that "money doesn't grow on trees," replacing it with "I attract money easily, as if it grows in my own backyard" might not feel true for you. Saying "I'm open to creating wealth in my life very easily" might feel more truthful and be easier for you to focus on.

Write out your new beliefs and commit to writing them every day. Post them somewhere you can see them like on your bathroom mirror or on the dashboard of your car. Read them aloud as often as possible to refocus on your positive and empowering money story.

MASTERING YOUR INNER GAME

Now that you've identified the unconscious stories that have been driving your actions around money (as well as your results), it's time for you to clean up your inner game so every part of you is aligned with creating more wealth. **That means making sure your conscious thoughts match your unconscious beliefs.** This makes it so much easier to take the actions needed to live a really wealthy life!

Now it's time to get a clear picture of what's been going on for you emotionally in response to these old stories. **By taking CONTROL of our focus, we reclaim our true power to produce the results we desire in life. Our beliefs are so powerful. By cleaning up our unconscious beliefs through this process, we stop the internal struggles that have been holding us back. By acknowledging difficult emotions, we release their** power over us. We get to DELETE these repetitive, controlling and unsupportive patterns that create resistance. Through this process, we get to ALTER the results we see in our life by changing our emotional responses and beliefs.

STEP 1:

You've already identified your old, unhelpful beliefs, so now it's time to get clear on the underlying emotions that have been unconsciously driving your actions (or lack of!). Relax and let all those old, Lack money stories and the emotions beneath them come to the surface. Even if you're unsure of the specific emotions, make a list of any you think could be lurking there – emotions like fear, discomfort, guilt, anxiety, shame etc. Take a deep breath and acknowledge these feelings.

STEP 2:

Decide to accept everything you've experienced up until now – all the highs and all the lows. Decide that you'll no longer allow these emotions to drive your behavior. Write a journal entry about how you feel while you acknowledge these emotions. You can tear it up or throw it in a fire as a symbol of letting these emotions go. Do it. Give yourself a pat on the back for doing this work and get excited about what your life will look like on the other side!

STEP 3:

Let's start developing skilled mastery of your inner game. Commit to staying aware of your emotional responses throughout the day. Notice how they're driving your actions in every moment. Decide not to judge yourself for anything you're feeling. Practicing acknowledging your emotions without judgement is such a powerful practice. It will give you the insight you need to start making shifts in your actions. Emotional mastery and building a supportive inner game will transform your life and your finances.

HOW YOUR PROGRAMMING IMPACTS YOUR MONEY MINDSET

Now it's time to go a little deeper. This will help you have a better understanding of how your money mindset works on a subconscious level. But I must warn you: This is the kind of important work that will support your process to lift the barriers to help you live your fullest life. Doing this work brings you one step closer to living out your God-given assignment!

There's even more good news – you can start to make changes **today**. The most important thing to remember is that the conscious mind is where you think your everyday thoughts – where you do all your wishing for change. It's your intellectual mind, your thinking mind. Your subconscious mind is where your old programs are running – often going against what you're thinking about. Your subconscious mind is where the feelings of resistance or conflict come in. Now that you're aware, let's make incremental changes. It's the little things you do that can make a big difference. What are you attempting to accomplish? What little thing can you do today that will make you more effective? You're probably only one step away from greatness.

How so? We're going to **CTRL, ALT, DEL. Your CONTROL is your internal focus (and the picture you have on the screen of your mind).** See yourself living in abundance and you'll attract it. It always works, it works every time with every person. If you're thinking of debt, that's what you're going to attract. Do you know what you think about most of the time? Take a look at the results you're getting, that will tell you exactly what's going on inside you. The subconscious mind can't tell the difference between what's real and what's imagined.

Understanding how this works gives you the power to change. Once you ALTER the thoughts you consciously choose – by picking ones that make you feel good – always ask yourself the question, "Is this going to help get me to my goal or not?"

Ask yourself this instead of thinking and ruminating on ones that make you feel bad – that's when you start seeing different results. This gives you the power to DELETE your current thought about your money set point, or income level, and move through resistance to a different level of income.

Step 1:

Write down the current results you're seeing in your financial life. Note all the facts, figures, patterns and behaviors you can identify. Be honest – I know it's not easy – but it's so worth it. This work will give you the clarity you need to set your three financial goals: yearly income, retirement income and savings income. This is the first important step to making real shifts in creating the money you need to live your most purposeful life. Imagine a life with no financial barriers!

Step 2:

Next write down what you think and feel about these results you've just identified. That will give you a clear indication of how you got this programming in the first place. See what memories or causes come up when you turn your attention to each of the results you've noticed. The good news is, it's not super important how you got them – but having some level of awareness is all you need to move forward with making the change.

Step 3:

Understand that all the money you need is available to you in every moment. Decide to take responsibility and maintain an awareness of how your programming is playing out to bring you these repetitive results in your day-to-day life. Having this active awareness allows you to choose a different result – **despite** the way you feel or habitually act. Moving forward with this new understanding allows you to choose to create a different result, instead of letting your old programs run the show!

SAY HELLO TO YOUR TRUE SELF

Congratulations for making it this far! A little fact check – you are brave for doing this work. Keep going! You now know that you have a choice about whether or not to let your old programs run things. You're starting to gain a deeper understanding of who you are and what you're capable of. You're not a victim. You have the power to take full responsibility for your life and you can create whatever you want. This power comes from your True Self (not your programming!). And now you're ready to learn how to tap into your True Self to see more opportunities around you to create wealth.

How? You guessed it… CTRL, ALT DEL.

Take CONTROL of the focus on which part of you is running the show (your programming or your True Self).

ALTER your outcomes by overriding your old programmed beliefs. Use your new awareness to take responsibility and change your actions…

You'll successfully DELETE a lot of your resistance and unwanted results for good!

Step 1:

Now that you're specifically aware of the unwanted results you've been creating with your subconscious programming, it's time to decide **how** you want to change these results. Your programing was created through repetition. So, you create a new program the same way, through repetition. Write down how exactly you'd like to change each one of the programs you've identified. How will you act going forward, in spite of your old programming? Daily, write out your new goal(s). Because, remember...

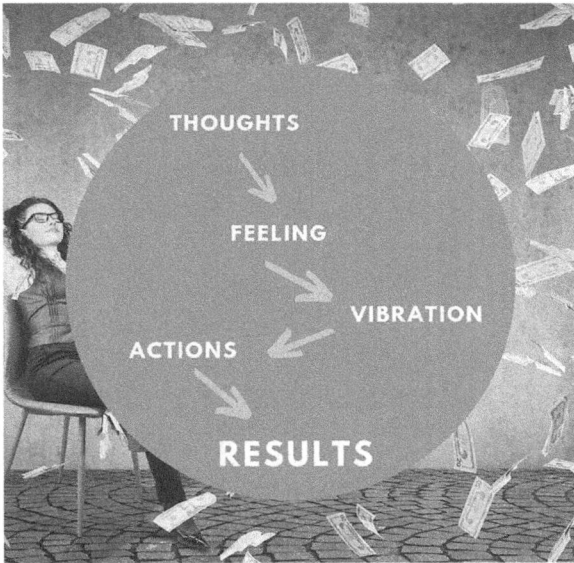

THOUGHTS

FEELING

VIBRATION

ACTIONS

RESULTS

Step 2:

Commit to noticing when you're feeling resistance or conflict. Remember that it's really the job of your subconscious mind to bring you more of the same... whatever you've been doing up until this point has kept you alive until now. When your mind comes up against something new... something unfamiliar and potentially unsafe... it can bring up feelings of conflict. When this happens, choose to move to a place of understanding. The secret to switching from feeling stuck to getting results, is taking action even though you have fear, and dealing with conflicting thoughts.

Step 3:

Your emotions are like your GPS system. Check your guidance system and alter the thought that is creating uncomfortable emotions. Be patient with yourself! The subconscious mind can't tell the difference between what's real and what's imagined. We can build anything in our imagination, that's where all creation begins in your life.

CHAPTER TWO

FEAR IS A LIAR

This book is all about YOU – about becoming a fuller, more vibrant, conscious and connected version of yourself. This book is about you being able to be fully you – unapologetically.

And when you are FULLY YOU – you serve your purpose – your greater truth. And when you serve your greater truth, you unlock all the prosperity that you could ever dream of experiencing.

I know in the last chapter, we talked about and began to work through your personal money story and your money blocks. But we only scratched the surface of money blocks and now it's time to grab the bull by the horns and talk about Fear. Yes, girl, Fear is such a big challenge in all of our lives that I had to devote an entire chapter to it!

Because fear is real. And it's especially real for us women. Fear is what keeps us from being our whole selves. Fear keeps us from creating a life we want… on our terms. Fear keeps us playing small and playing safe. So, we're going to work to understand fear and how it's keeping us from what we really want and, more importantly, how to overcome it.

You can't wish harder or say a million affirmations without dealing with the real stuff, and admit the underlying truth that feels scary, but is actually incredibly liberating.

The personal development industry tells you that you have to **fake** being positive, and that you have to be 100% focused on the good stuff.

But the truth is that does you a disservice because you never deal with nasty, real fears and feelings underneath, and that's where the true gold is.

GIRL, WHAT'S HOLDING YOU BACK?

You already know, but I think it's worth mentioning again – women are amazing! We hold it down – for our families, our community and the world! There's one thing I see across the board for the majority of us – because we have so many roles, are conditioned to play it safe, and are often times told that we have to choose –I see certain conditions/philosophies/self-sabotaging behaviors holding us back. These are very general and can apply to any area of our lives (including money, but I'll address specific fears involving money momentarily). Ready to find out what they are?

Ok, here are the top five things that holds most women back:

Waiting for "The Stars to Align"

How many times have you thought, "the timing for this just isn't right," and that keeps being your answer every time you think about changes you know you need to make? Truth is there's never going to be a perfect time to start. There's always going to be something else that comes up. If you're still waiting for that perfect time to start may never come. Start taking imperfect actions.

Guilt

As women, we tend to put ourselves last and are reluctant to do anything that might seem indulgent or selfish, because we'll feel guilty. You should never feel guilty about making decisions that will ultimately improve your future. Try to rid yourself of the thought that if you "rock the boat, my friends and family will leave me behind."

Insecurity

Stepping outside your comfort zone is hard. We don't believe we're good enough, qualified, or feel we need more degrees etc. As women, we're passing on opportunities because we feel unsure – when the reality is we do have what it takes. By owning our power instead of hiding from it, we find strength we didn't know we had, but it's there in all of us.

Not Asking for Help

Overwhelm can result in unwanted stress in your life. No one can do it all, all by ourselves, and it rarely ends well when we try to do so. But somehow, we've convinced ourselves that we're not smart or capable enough if we ask for help. We see it as weakness. Quite the contrary! Once you reach out to people for help, things became a lot easier. The funny thing is, people often don't mind being asked to help and find it empowering and rewarding.

Impatience

We all want things to happen right now. And some days, it becomes difficult to stand in the moment and wait. Celebrating your small wins is a true turning point during those impatient times.

BUT REALLY, WHAT IS FEAR?

So, what is fear? The dictionary describes fear as "as an unpleasant emotion caused by threat of danger, pain or harm." As adults, we often relegate fear to objects or things, but never seek to investigate further. Such as "fear of flying" or "fear of spiders."

I came across a very relevant definition of fear that I'd like to share with you:

FALSE EVIDENCE APPEARING REAL

Here's the thing – many of us have been down this path of personal development before – and these trainings will either reinforce what you've already learned or introduce you to thought patterns you need to interrupt in order to transform.

Fears come in all shapes and sizes, and varying depths of intensity. No two people will demonstrate the same type of fear to the same thing. That's one of the reasons facing your fear can be so difficult. But what is common with fear is that it holds women back. Addressing our fears can be hard, and as women who are minding our businesses, not properly working through our fears blocks the momentum we need to take our businesses and lives to the next level.

What does fear gotta do with money?

Money is an emotional subject and one that we don't like talking about. Yet it impacts all areas of our lives – how we live and how we spend our time. Fears associated with money activate our reptilian brain (there's that science stuff, again). Even though we aren't living in the wild and hunting and gathering our food (and watching a tiger in the bush), our brain is wired to go on high alert to any threat. If we feel fearful about money, we'll naturally avoid it because this is how we're wired. I like to say the only way out is through.

In my line of work, I talk about fear of money more often than I'd like. I'd much rather talk about the abundance of it – the opportunities money creates by having more of it. But many women tell me they're afraid of numbers or math or money, and therefore they generally ignore their finances. Some have confided that they're afraid to look under the hood at their own financial situation for fear of seeing how bad it actually is. Remember, the action you take as a result of how you think and feel gives you the results you have in your life today. Consider this – money will have a greater influence on your life than almost any other commodity you can think of.

You must begin to understand that the present state of your bank account, your sales, your health, your social life, your position at work, etc. is nothing more than the physical manifestation of your previous thinking.

Doubts, fears, pessimism and negative thinking poison the very source of life. They sap energy, enthusiasm, ambition, hope, faith and everything else which makes life purposeful, joyful and creative.

Ergo, what you believe about money is what you'll create in your life.

Looking at our numbers is actually what can help us take better financial care of our family and ourselves. Money loves attention just like any relationship you have in life. *See yourself living in abundance and you will attract it. It always works, it works every time with every person.*

COMMON MONEY FEARS

The way to get out of fear is to take small action steps:
fear + action = courage.

1. **Fear of becoming a Bag Lady – "Bag lady, you gon' hurt your back..."** This is the number one fear most women have, and it's a real syndrome. It's the fear that we'll be broke and homeless as we age and not able to afford medical care. According to the 2013 Women, Money & Power Study from insurer Allianz Life, 50 percent of American women fear becoming a "bag lady." This fear spans all types of women even 27 percent of women in the study earning more

than $200,000 per year. The study shows that after the fear of losing a spouse, running out of money in retirement is what keeps 57 percent of women up at night. The average woman aged 65 lives six years longer than the average man. As a result, she's typically widowed and living alone. What we resist will persist and in fact it will make you even more anxious. Start today by doing one small thing to give one area of your finances your attention.

2. **No thanks, my spouse/partner handles that.** This is a common practice with women. Women tend to live an average of five to six years longer than their spouses. At some point, we'll be on our own and we'll have to face our finances. This point was driven home recently when a friend of mine suddenly lost her husband. Losing a spouse is not the time to take over finances.

3. **Money marriage problems.** Not talking about finances can lead to a divided marriage. Maybe one of you is a spender and the other is a saver. Those are two very different money personalities. If you have a spouse or partner, start talking about finances.

4. **You're afraid to look at your bills or bank statements.** You think avoiding looking at your bills is better than knowing what you owe or have or don't have in the bank. Face your fear – to make money you must give it attention on a daily or weekly basis. Not knowing or looking at what you have in your accounts, or how much you owe actually leads to more anxiety and fear. Get a trusted person – a friend or a financial adviser, banker or accountant – to help you review and interpret your financial documents. The more often you look at your finances, the more motivated you will be to do something about it.

5. **Fear of Math** – We all have lots of excuses – "I'm not good with math and my mind goes into overwhelm looking at budgets." This is a fear disguised as an excuse. Here's how the mind works with fear: We over complicate things or procrastinate – this is a form of fear. Take small steps toward what you fear most – this is a way to desensitize yourself. Make looking at your finances a positive experience, put on calming music, light a candle, sit down and look at your bills or your expenses. If you can sort out what you "need" to pay each month to support your lifestyle or business, this is a good first step. Then you know how much you need to make each month just to have the basics covered. After your needs are taken care of, you can add in things that you

want such as a health club membership or salon haircuts. If making a budget for the year is too much, start with a monthly budget. The point is to face the fear of budgeting and start now.

6. **Fear of asserting your worth.** Traditionally, women were socialized to put our needs last. I believe that women in general weren't taught how to talk about money, how to make money and how to budget. I recommend you start now. Some women fear that if they ask for a raise they might get fired. Negotiation is a skill you want to learn now.

7. **Undervaluing your worth or giving your services away for free.** The biggest mistake I see new entrepreneurs make is to price their services by the hour. People will hire you because they have a problem they need to solve. Ask yourself, what's it worth to them to have that problem solved? What will it cost them not to have this problem solved? Always focus on the value you provide them.

8. **Partner Fears.** When I grew up, my mom would go shopping at bargain stores and then hide the purchases from my stepdad. I've done that in the past, but I no longer do this. When we're aware and understand what we're doing – if it's not a positive behavior – then we can take action to make a change – that's transformation. Honesty is the basis for a solid relationship. It starts first with being honest with yourself.

9. **Emergency, say what?** Women worry they don't have enough money to save for an emergency fund. If you start saving even $25 a month automatically out of your paycheck or when you pay yourself first in your business, put a small amount in a savings account. Make this a habit and as the years go by, you'll have an emergency account.

10. **Retirement, say what?** This can be a paralyzing fear and it's the same situation as not having an emergency fund. If you start today, I promise you'll feel better about it. Start with any amount you can save and make this a monthly habit.

"Progress is impossible without change, and those who cannot change their minds cannot change anything."
– George Bernard Shaw

Do any of these common fears that drive behavior about money ring a bell for you? Let's look at how fear and fear about money are creating some pretty toxic, self-limiting beliefs that are holding you back from explosive growth in your business or career. They are usually generalisations about the past based on our own interpretations. The challenge comes when we need to identify these beliefs as just that – beliefs! Beliefs that we created and that are NOT the truth.

When we don't know or acknowledge our fears, they continue to live in your brain; wreaking havoc on your mind, body and ultimately your prosperity.

Calling a thing a thing gives you dominion over it. **Calling a thing a thing, will help you identity and eliminate what's preventing your from taking radical action for your life!**

Let's look at a long (but unfortunately, not exhaustive) list of limiting beliefs I've either held myself, or I've helped countless women overcome.

> *"Beliefs have the power to create and the power to destroy."*
>
> **– Anthony Robbins-**

ISOLATING AND CONQUERING YOUR MAJOR FEARS

In order to understand and work through your fears, you need to isolate them one at a time. Start with one that really interferes with your growth. You don't feel good enough? You don't make enough money? You're not smart? You aren't pretty enough? You aren't lovable?

Girl, it's time to get your journal out again! Look at the statements below, and check those that really resonate with you.

After you choose, ask yourself "why" for each statement, repeating this question as many times as you can until you run out of answers.

The last answer is usually the root cause. But you have to be painfully honest with yourself to find and kill off that root cause.

- [ ] I have not really made the authentic choice to be fully alive and engaged in life for the rest of my life.

- [ ] I need to be right.

- [ ] I am not clear on my personal values or I am not living in alignment with them.

☐ I am addicted or attached to substances, people or behaviors.

☐ I am currently living a big lie.

☐ I really don't have anything better to do with my life right now.

☐ I have financial problems or other major lifestyle concerns.

☐ I am missing key, empowering relationships in my life.

☐ My needs are not being met.

☐ My life is primarily about me and my problems.

☐ I don't get how life works so well for other people but not for me.

☐ I have not experienced very much in life yet. My life is boring.

☐ I am under a lot of stress.

☐ I don't take care of myself or my health the way I should.

Identifying and understanding the root cause opens the door for addressing fears.

UPLEVEL FROM FEAR TO COURAGE

"How you gonna win if you ain't right within?"

– Lauryn Hill

One of the things we must do as Christian career-centered or business owning women is **work our fear so we can level up to courage**. What I mean by that is identifying your fear, understanding your fear, and taking certain steps to address and overcome it will move you to a place of courage. It doesn't not mean you are **fearless**, it means:

You are courageous. You are brave.

Fear is real, but what you may be afraid of **may not be real**. The reason you aren't moving forward is because your fears are greater than your desire. Please write it down. Fear stimulates your brain which releases chemicals. These chemicals cause physical symptoms that we're all familiar with – racing heartbeat, quickness of breath, tightening of muscles. But this chemical release also does something else to you – it triggers your **fight or flight response**. As an entrepreneur or career-focused woman, this translates to "I stopped," or "I didn't finish," or "I delayed or procrastinated," – **flight response.**

Or

"I kept at it," or "I completed it," or "I was ride or die," – **fight response.**

Because your brain is complex, your brain's neurons, the communication pathways for **everything** we sense, think and do, automatically control your body's response.

So, even when you're reacting and conscious, you can't change the reaction unless you **choose to change the reaction.**

There's a **major** difference between "There's a fire," and "I'm running from a fire." The brain doesn't know the difference, it's just responding to a perceived threat. It's like quick brain and slow brain. Quick brain allows you to react automatically without much thought so you can remove yourself from danger.

Slow brain is your discernment filter. It allows you to rationalize, investigate, intuit and adjust.

For the purpose of driving this point home, let's switch to the negative mindset and downsides of becoming wealthier. Let's talk about the negative consequences of you becoming wealthier and achieving everything on your dream board. Unconsciously, you are **fearing** the unintended, negative consequences of your goals.

You think there could be downsides that outweigh the positives so you hold yourself back and unconsciously sabotage yourself from taking action.

When you uncover the negative consequences, acknowledge them, and if necessary **plan** for them, you are on the road to achieving your goals.

DEVELOPING A HAPPY, HEALTHY, COMMITTED RELATIONSHIP WITH MONEY

So why did I go through all of that? Well, as the title of this chapter connotes – fear will keep you stuck. And it's screwing up your best life, girl! You might not have realized it yet, but self-belief and money are intertwined. *When you struggle with one, you invariably struggle with the other.*

Don't believe me? For example…

If you don't believe in yourself – your gifts, talents or purpose –your financial situation will always be less than what you want it to be. On a subconscious level, you think you don't actually deserve money. You might think you aren't good enough at your job, and that you aren't worthy of earning more. You might even feel guilty for asking people to pay for your services because your self-doubt is so incredibly high.

Struggle inside always translates to struggle outside.

Money and fear are so intimately connected that when money is lacking or is abundant, you begin to think negatively about yourself!

You constantly worry about judgement or scorn from others. Having "too much" money means you're greedy or undeserving of such abundance, and you look for ways to quickly part with it. Not having enough money connotes you're lazy and irresponsible. All of these scenarios can devilishly play subconsciously.

You're caught in a never-ending cycle, shadow-boxing with yourself and the world, which leaves you tired and frustrated. All you want to do is to help people and make a difference.

Please believe me when I tell you that I can relate to those feelings. You wonder how you're able to make such a profound difference in other people's lives while you have such a complicated relationship with money yourself.

Remember… **your love for yourself is expressed through creating a stable relationship with your money**. You can't have wealth in your material world until you have first visualized wealth in your mind.

Prosperity and abundance properly understood are simply the inward awareness of the opulence, wholeness and completeness that abounds within the spiritual realm.

Your abundance has been waiting for you the whole time. God has been waiting to give it to you. He's just been waiting for you to say "I am safe," and **"Yes, God, thank you! It's okay for me to have money."**

I hope you're just as excited as I am to take your power back, acknowledge your fears, master your inner game and **handle your money, honey!**

CHAPTER THREE

WHAT IS LOVE?
BABY DON'T HURT ME....

By now, you're probably noticing a theme in this book. That's not only by my design, but by Divine Design. Just in case you missed it, I'll repeat it again: **self-love and money are intertwined. When you struggle with one, you invariably struggle with the other.**

But how can you even talk about self-love, if we don't talk about self-image first?

Self-worth is at the basis of our very selves – our thoughts, feelings and behaviors are intimately tied to how we view our worthiness and value as a human being.

When you look in the mirror, you think the image staring back at you is it. That's who you are. But while your physical body and appearance are important, it's the self-image that's locked in your subconscious mind that really counts. **This** is the image that determines your success or failure in life.

When you're looking in the mirror, the mirror doesn't tell you the real you is perfect, boundless and is always looking for ways to expand. No, the mirror only reflects what you physically see. That physical image is cloaking the self-image in your mind. This self-image is based on false and limited information that sets boundaries for every area of your life such as:

1. Appearance – whether that's the number on the scale, the size of clothing worn, or the attention received by others

2. Net worth – this can mean income, material possessions, financial assets or all of the above

3. Who you know/your social circle – some people judge their own value and the value of others by their status and what important and influential people they know

4. What you do/your career – people are often judged by what they do; for example, a stockbroker is usually considered more successful and valuable than a janitor or a teacher

5. What you achieve – as noted earlier, we frequently use achievements to determine someone's worth (whether it's our own worth or someone else's), such as success in business, SAT scores, or placement in a marathon or other athletic challenge (Morin, 2017).

This is wrong. Everything you're using to measure your image is a lie.

If you see yourself as shy, not good enough or unlovable, you'll feel and act accordingly. That will create results in your outer world that reflect the image you have in your mind. But we measure the value our self-image on pure superficial results in the physical world such as:

1. Your to-do list: achieving goals is great and it feels wonderful to cross things off your list, but that doesn't have a direct relationship with your worth as a human

2. Your job: it doesn't matter what you do; what matters is that you do it well and that it fulfills you

3. Your social media following: it also doesn't matter how many people think you are worthy of a follow or a retweet; it can be enlightening and healthy to consider the perspectives of others, but their opinions have no impact on our innate value

4. Your age: you aren't too young or too old for anything; your age is simply a number and doesn't factor into your value as a human being

5. Other people: as noted above, it doesn't matter what other people think or what other people have done or accomplished; your personal satisfaction and fulfillment is much more important than what others are thinking, saying, or doing

6. How far you can run: your mile run-time is one of the least important factors for your self-worth (or for anything else, for that matter); if you enjoy running and feel fulfilled by improving your time, good for you! If not, good for you! Your ability to run does not determine your self-worth.

7. Your grades: we all have different strengths and weaknesses, and some of us are simply not cut out for class; this has no bearing on our value as people, and a straight-A student is just as valuable and worthy as a straight-F student or a dropout.

8. The number of friends you have: your value as a human has absolutely nothing to do with how many friends or connections you have; the quality of your relationships is what's really important.

9. Your relationship status: whether flying solo, casually dating or in a committed relationship, your value is exactly the same – your relationship status doesn't alter your worth

10. The money (or lack thereof) in the bank: if you have enough money to physically survive (which can, in fact, be $0), then you have already achieved the maximal amount of "worth" you can get from money

11. Your likes: it doesn't matter if you have "good taste" or not, if your friends and acquaintances think you're sophisticated, or if you have an eye for the finer things; your worth is the same regardless

12. Anything or anyone but yourself: here we get to the heart of the matter – you are the only one who determines your self-worth. If you believe you're worthy and valuable, you're worthy and valuable. Even if you don't believe you're worthy and valuable, guess what – you're still worthy and valuable!

Have you been using some of the lame criteria above to determine your self-worth? Do you feel like you're enough? If not, how can you love yourself? Girl, no one is ever going to love you more than you love yourself. But even if you promise yourself that you're going to do something different, you won't deviate from that pattern. At least not for long because your self-image is on autopilot. Seriously. I'll give you an example.

Let's suppose that your self-image is that you're overweight. It might not be something you ever talk about, but inside you feel you're overweight.

One day, you get tired of feeling that way, and you decide to do something about it – you change your diet, work out like crazy and begin to lose weight.

Hurray! Done! You've created a new habit for the better. Done and done. But not really. Here's why: You were not overweight simply because of the foods you're eating and lack of exercise (that's only one piece of a much larger puzzle). You were overweight because of the overweight image you're holding in your subconscious mind. That image causes you to hold on to extra pounds. If you had a "skinny" self-image, you could eat all the foods you like, including things like chocolate. Then, whenever you overeat, you'd simply pass off the extra food – what's not needed to manifest the image that's in your mind.

The bottom line is that when you, as an overweight person, decided to go on a diet without altering your self-image, any weight loss will be temporary. The self-image, which is on autopilot, will continue to operate as such until you decide to CTRL-ALT-DEL and adopt a new self-image.

THREE CONSEQUENCES OF LOW SELF-IMAGE

You may be asking, "Choyo, if it's that simple, then why do we do this to ourselves and live this way?" The answer to that question is astonishingly easy: We live that way because we don't know any different. We think it's normal to stay in our lane and blend in with the crowd.

Ladies, you know you don't want to or have to live like this! To change this, you have to learn to keep your mind on a higher image rather than a lower concern. I know it's **not** an easy thing to do, but it sure pays great dividends for the person who develops the mental strength to do it.

When you change how you see yourself in your conscious mind and plant the idea in your subconscious mind, it changes your vibration (we talked about this earlier). Then the conditions and circumstances in your life automatically change. Look at how having a negative self-image will negatively impact your life and your relationship with money:

Feeling Pretty Crappy About Yourself. A problem arises when you use money as the value or yardstick for your measure of self-worth. You deem yourself not good enough solely because your cash balance or your ability to make an income is low.

In addition, driven by the fears of your ego, you can't help but compare yourself to your friends. Invariably, you feel lousy about yourself; you wonder why manifesting what they want is so easy for them. You label yourself a failure for not attaining financial success. Needless to say, a lack in confidence can prevent you from clenching that sale or making a business breakthrough.

Not Open to Receiving. Unfortunately, a low self-image makes you a poor receiver. As a poor receiver, you're not aligned with universal abundance (which rests on the giving-receiving circuit of energy exchange). And guess what? You become closed to what the Universe has to offer to you.

Think of it this way. **God may already be sending tons of resources, ideas and connections your way; but vibrationally, you are saying "no" to these because you believe you're unworthy.** These resources, ideas and connections can potentially lead you to building net worth. However, since you're not open to receive, the Universe may just send them over to your friends (or enemies) – who **are** open to receive – instead!

Unable to Charge What You Are Truly Worth. If you're an entrepreneur, or have aspirations of being one, low self-worth can have an impact if you provide any form of service. With low self-worth, you won't be able to charge what you're worth. You simply can't do it. Thus, you charge a price that is below the market, despite the ton of value you provide. You end up with an energy leakage and possibly feeling resentful about yourself and your situation. Your self-love quotient reduces with every anger spear you hurl at yourself.

CULTIVATING SELF-WORTH AND SELF IMAGE

So now that you're beginning to understand that the foundation to crafting a happy, fulfilling life is rooted in understanding oneself. Your self-worth (and self-image) define who you think you are, how you value yourself and how you fit into the world. Your personal identity includes personality traits, beliefs, emotions, and characteristics that help to define each individual person. It is purely internal.

It applies to everyone, because everyone is going to have some kind of belief about who or what they are. For example, say you are a person who believes that you are quirky and unique and rebellious, so you are going to broadcast to the world, whether through words or deeds, that you are a rebellious and unique. You send a clear message (narrative) about the person you believe yourself to be.

Understanding your current self-worth and self-image narrative and creating a new one requires undertaking some intentional exercises. Don't worry, I've outlined some of my favorites below.

"A self is not something static, tied up in a pretty parcel and handed to the child, finished and complete. A self is always becoming."
– Madeleine L'Engle

Shake it Like a (Mental) Polaroid Picture

A person who believes in themselves and puts forward a strong sense of self-worth is more likely to act and move positively and attract positive treatment. So why not develop and hold a positive view of self-worth and self-image in the first place?

Do you know what the most powerful tool we have at our disposal? Our imaginations. This is why visioning is so key to life – **everything we do is preceded by an image. We think first in order to form an image, then we do the work.**

Your vision is your most important mental Polaroid picture. This mental Polaroid picture inspires you and gives you energy and unlocks your deepest motivations. Remember that you that you have great resources of talent and ability locked up, within you, just waiting to be expressed. Your mental Polaroid picture is connection between your truest self and your everyday behaviors, thus making you unstoppable!

To create your own mental Polaroid pictures, I want you to create the images of your ideal life in your mind and watch what happens. Snap! In your mind's eye, I want you to create images of yourself in a much more abundant state of life. Girl, it sounds so simple, and it really is. Please trust me on this one – see yourself already in possession of what you previously only dreamed of. Remember, you are the Co-Creator with God – your entire life, your being is not only filled with and surrounded by everything that started with images.

For this exercise, I recommend getting an journal or a legal pad. Right now, (yes girl, like RIGHT NOW) build the mental Polaroid pictures in your mind of yourself already in possession of abundance and prosperity. Build the mental Polaroid picture of what you are doing, what you look like, how you act and how others see you – your most capable, creative and free self! Now, write brief descriptions of these mental Polaroid pictures in the present tense in your journal. Make sure you get VERY detailed. Then minimize everything you wrote. Think about it like something you would put on a billboard. And carry it in your purse. Read it every day, a number of times, until the image fills your consciousness.

If you need help, use the following writing prompt:

Snap! In this Polaroid picture, I see myself:

_____

_____

_____

_____

_____

_____

Snap! In this Polaroid picture, I feel....

_____

_____

_____

_____

_____

Snap! In this Polaroid picture, I'm taking massive action towards my goal

_____

_____

_____

_____

_____

Snap! Today is so awesome! In this Polaroid picture, you can see how unique and special I am because I...

_____

_____

_____

_____

_____

SELF-LOVE AS A WEAPON AGAINST LOW SELF-WORTH

Now that you've worked on creating the ultimate mental Polaroid picture of yourself and your life, you can begin to foster it with love and care for yourself, AKA self-love. Make it a goal to extend yourself kindness, tolerance, generosity and compassion.

Self-love is your secret weapon to living a fulfilling life. That's because your inner world creates your outer world. The concept of self-love is Divinely grounded in the premise that you must accept and love yourself without conditions. This kind of love expresses a quality of spirit, allowing you to embrace your shortcomings and doubts by acknowledging your individual strengths and what some call weaknesses, but what I prefer to call "areas for potential growth," without judgment.

Let me say it again: **Before you can receive love and respect from others, you need to love and respect yourself.**

Self-love is being our best friend through all the difficulties in life, not only when everything is going well. We crave the kind of nurturing love we expect a parent to have for a child and if you never received this as children, you now need to parent yourselves, to be loving, nurturing and accepting, especially during difficult times. As this process starts to unfold, we'll feel safe and the barriers between ourselves and others will diminish.

When you make decisions out of guilt, a need to please or avoid conflict, you overvalue the needs of others and disrespect yourself.

Love begets love, so you're drawn to give to others. You have the energy to give and in turn, giving energizes you.

Do you love yourself? What does self-love mean to you? How do you show yourself that you love yourself?

> *"Wealth is the product of man's capacity to think."*
>
> **– Ayn Rand**

It's about the money, but it's never just about the money

By now, you're getting yourself pretty familiar (and somewhat comfortable, I hope) in acknowledging your specific themes and money blocks that are simmering just below the surface. Until this point, you've probably gone through life without recognizing how much these deeper issues fuel your money challenges (and successes). Before you know that money is never just about the money, working with it can feel like emotional quicksand. A simple evening of paying bills spins out of control into self-doubt, shame and a volcano of unresolved family trauma. You might even feel like you'll never resolve all this messy "money stuff."

But you want to create wealth. That's one of the reasons you're reading this book. On some level, you've recognized that you still aren't living your best life and that your level of wealth plays a big part in that. So, here we are.

But, you absolutely must understand money is not the goal in creating wealth. Let me repeat that: **money is not the goal**. As a therapist, when I work with people to get through life's challenges and meet their goals, one of the recurring topics is people telling me they want to make money. I know it's not money they're really after. It's the things money can buy and the freedom of time to do what they really want. I know this sounds like the same thing, but there's a difference, and knowing (or not knowing) this difference is actually the reason so many people never become wealthy.

Back to the mechanics of your money relationship. For many people, their relationship with money is like a torrid love affair – a nasty love/hate situation. Money, as an object, is neither good nor bad. It's only bad when it's lacking, restricted or hoarded. These restrictions create outcomes that exploit people and the planet. These restrictions and the utilization of money to support these restrictions that create and reinforce negative associations.

You've already started exploring your money relationship. Your money relationship has imprints that highlight:

1. Your relationship to pleasure, abundance and thriving

2. How you access feelings of enoughness and safety

3. Your capacity to feel worthy and valuable

4. Your self-confidence, self-reliance and resilience

5. Your ability to get vulnerable, get intimate and ask for help

6. Your capacity to understand your purpose and ability/willingness to live in your purpose

Money always mirrors our unresolved issues, suppressed gifts and growth patterns.

MONEY, YOUR PURPOSE AND CONNECTEDNESS

Here's the clincher: money, your purpose and connectedness are all inextricably linked. Yep, never separated. The concept that they are is a myth. No, a lie.

Our sense of separation from each other is at the root of all our human conflicts. However, the greatest sense of separation, the one that actually leads to all the rest, is our fundamental sense of separation from God. I will suggest, in fact, this is the only real problem we have – our sense of separation from God. To be separated from God is to be separated from our purpose. The belief that we can thrive and be successful despite being separated from God and our purpose, is the primary cause behind all acts of violence and cruelty, to ourselves and others, all wars, and all destruction of our beautiful planet. The only solution to our personal and global problems is to come back to a realization of our oneness with our Heavenly Father; life itself and all that entails.

If you're still not following me, consider this: When the bible says, "I and my father are one, and all that the father has is mine.… the cattle on a thousand hills… the earth and the fullness thereof…" it's speaking of this realization of oneness with the fountain of all creation. When it talks about the Prodigal Son who leaves his father's house, takes his inheritance, and tries to make it on his own, only to become broke and broken and finally return home again, it's describing our human journey of leaving our sense of oneness with the source of creation, creating a separate sense of existence that leads to all the pain and suffering and beginning our journey back home to oneness. This is also the meaning behind the metaphor of the vine and its branches, and how a human is like a branch cut off from the vine or tree, which withers and dies. Once you understand this principle, if you go back and read the great scriptures of the world (from all religions), you'll start to see what they're really teaching. It boils down to this: we're dreaming that we are separate from God –and we need to wake up and stay awake to realize our oneness again.

As long as we're operating from separation, and therefore lacking in our purpose, true wealth and fulfillment will always be 'out there' no matter how much we have.

MONEY AND MENTAL ENERGY

Imagine who you could become if you knew that all wealth and abundance was within you, infinite, inexhaustible and unconditional, merely awaiting your activation and expression. This is not only possible, it is divinely designed to be this way.

So many of us are trapped in the thinking of "**I have to see it, believe it to receive it. I have to receive it to achieve it.**" This ridiculous philosophy has caused so much pain and frustration as so many well-intentioned, brilliant women have put their lives on the layaway plan thinking they couldn't go for what they wanted until they believed in themselves or the goal enough. In other words, until they felt good about it, worthy of it, confident they could do it, or at least not afraid. While our state of feeling and belief is certainly a powerful force, it isn't necessary to go for what we want, ask for what we want, or in many cases, actually get what we want. Often just acting or asking opens the channels for receiving, or activates an inner feeling that starts generating the necessary energy to bring it to fruition. Snapping out of this hypnotic spell frees you from this waiting game and gets you into bold action toward your vision of awakened wealth.

Again, so many of us believe the lie of seeing is believing, that when we don't achieve what we want (focused on the results), we get demotivated, disenchanted, thinking that something is missing. My answer to that is whatever's missing is a sneak peek of what we're not giving to others – the world. We are divine power plants, and a power plant doesn't receive energy – or even have energy – it generates it. **Remember CTRL, ALT, DEL?** We have to actively shift our mental energy regardless of what our previous results are and believe our achievement is there, available and attained **anyway**. I call it active believing and it's akin to active imagination – generating new energy that accelerates our more empowered belief or completely shatters the old one.

When the ancient spiritual texts say 'Ask and you shall receive,' it's pointing us to this powerful principle. The reason this works is because everything is already here, already happening in the quantum field or spiritual reality. Even more, it's actively seeking outlets for its expression. The act of asking opens the channel to receive what is always being given. Let's practice this active believing and getting into the habit of creating positive, mental energy around money.

In this simple exercise, every time you participate in a transaction, instead of focusing on the money being exchanged – whether you're giving or receiving – **bring your attention to the energy behind the exchange**. For example, if you're filling your car with gas (or whatever fuel you prefer, including electricity), contemplate all the many people and aspects of creation that went into bringing you that fuel. The attendees at the filling station, the people who built that station, the truck drivers that delivered the fuel, the business people who managed all the administrative details, the executives who run the companies involved and all the many industries, resources and people that are required to find and extract the oil, build and run the refineries or power stations, mine the raw materials that are turned into all the equipment, and even all the farmers and grocers that harvest and sell the food that feeds all these people! Expanding even further, you begin to realize that all of nature, indeed the whole universe, has conspired in a grand circle of life to bring this fuel to you.

As you bring all of this into your awareness, consciously give thanks to everyone and everything that is part of this circle of life, love, support and supply. Bless it all. Feel the perfection of it all. Feel and sense how there really is only one life and one omni-activity appearing as many expressions of diversity. Allow yourself to expand into a sense of awe and wonder at it all. Breathe and let that feeling expand to fill your being. Let it loosen any places where you might feel separate, where you're holding on, believing you're in control.

Breathe and receive this enormous gift of grace that life is, recognizing that you didn't personally do anything to earn all of this, and there's no way you ever could. You didn't set up all the systems allow this fuel to get to you. You didn't create those farms or raise those farmers or teach those truck drivers or drill for oil or mine the raw materials. It wasn't your time, energy or education that made all that happen. No single person, no matter how brilliant they are, could ever begin to create, master or manage such a diverse, complex system – all of which is required to deliver your fuel, only grace has made it so.

As you rest in this grace, turn your attention to all the ways this fuel serves you, your family, friends and loved ones. See all the possibilities it gives you.

You can drive to a job that employees you, pick up your children from school, take your family on a fun vacation, explore and experience the world, deliver your gifts and so much more. Expand and increase your vision to imagine all the ripple effects of your activities. For example, because you can bring your child to school, they can become an educated citizen who then goes out into the world and contributes. Because you can go to work, you can give gifts that help all the people your business serves and earn money to support your family and all their endeavors. If you run out of ways this fuel blesses you, imagine all the other ways it blesses, allowing firefighters, police officers, paramedics and other service people to help those in need, save lives and keep the peace. Truly the blessings of this one thing are far and wide.

As you imagine all these different benefits, allow yourself to feel the qualities of it – the love, peace, joy, inspiration and gratitude. Really feel it all. Feel how abundant and blessed you are. Breathe and let that energy expand to fill your entire body, then breathe and radiate it out to the world, blessing everyone and everything.

Feel how the more you pay attention to it and share it, the more of this feeling and energy you have. That feeling tone of abundance, gratitude and joy is the real activity of wealth within you. As you practice this process, you'll start to fall more in love with the energy and qualities behind the outer symbols, until that's where you are predominantly living. **When you live more in the invisible energy of life, you have more and more access to the real substance of all creation – and your outer world expands to express this unlimited abundance.**

This is just one small area of your life, the fuel you put in your car. You could do it around the food that fuels your body, books, programs and other things that feed your mind, and anything else that nourishes your heart and soul or those you love.

There's virtually no end to how many ways you can practice tapping into the energy of abundance behind every form and experience. As you do this, you turn every transaction into a potential transformation. You become free of attachment to the outer things and a wide-open channel for a never-ending flow of good in your life.

MONEY AND SELF-CARE

Self-care is such a popular topic now that all you need to do is Google or better yet, open Instagram or Pinterest, you'll find plenty of examples of routines, rituals and affirmations. Luckily, I don't have to cover that in much detail. If you exercise or meditate regularly, or treat yourself to a relaxing bath or a movie night when you need restoration, you're probably familiar with the benefits of self-care. To be honest, self-care is not a one and done thing, it's something that requires plenty of practice and evolution based on your own needs and desires, and only you know those. You're an individual with unique interests and needs. If you follow my mantra for self-love, I'm incredibly confident that you'll be able to establish and grow a routine that leaves you feeling refreshed, nurtured and recharged.

There's one aspect glaringly missing from the examples of self-care. You guessed it, finances. Come on, this is a money mindset book! It's only befitting that I impress the importance of not only recharging yourself physically, mentally, emotionally, spiritually and intellectually, but also financially.

In order to create a self-care ritual that feels like it's yours very important to first define what self-care looks and feels like for you. Here, I'll even help you get started:

1. Do you understand the difference between selfish vs. a reflection of self-love?

2. What are you honestly willing to do to ensure you show up, more days than not, able to operate at maximum capacity because your soul is fed.

3. What will it take for you to view self-care not just as something you do on occasion to pamper yourself, but as something you practice every day? (This is a touchy one, so think long and hard and be honest with yourself)

Why are these questions important? Well, can you imagine if we all did a better job of not confusing self-love with being selfish? Imagine the impact that would have in your home and beyond! What's more, imagine if everyone (a) was taught the power of self-care, in general, and (b) practiced it as it pertained to how they manage their choices around money, too?

MONEY AS A SELF-CARE RITUAL

Money Practice

"Everything I do, on an ongoing basis, to help bring more clarity, peace of mind, and success to my money relationship. Something that helps me maintain my money relationship as a steadfast and supportive part of my life."

– Bari Tessler

I love Bari Tessler's definition of money practice because it puts the focus on money and its holistic relationship with you and your environment. It takes the sterility out of financial planning, and acknowledges the emotional aspect of money. A regular money practice will do wonders for your financial world. By tracking your income, spending and savings, you can wield more conscious control over this area of your life and align it ever more closely with your values. But the benefits don't stop there. Engaging with your money regularly can help you bolster your self-esteem, deepen your sense of safety and strengthen your intimate relationships.

So how do you develop a successful money practice? Well for one, treat it like you treat any of your healthy relationships. You engage consistently and regularly with your money practice because doing so nurtures your finances. Remember how you do money is how you do everything. So let's develop a healthy respect for money. Money goes where money is invited and stays where it is welcomed. As important as the "what" part of a money practice is, the "how" we do it is even more critical. Remember that there's no set way, do what feels right to you. When I experience any uncomfortable emotions around money that can be destructive. I first become very aware of the emotions. It's important to check how I'm feeling in the moment. Whenever negative emotions arise I switch to a more empowering emotion. I call this my switching strategies. I asked myself a question: what would I love? I think read my goal card, I visualize the outcome that I want and I connect to the feeling of its already being done. Sometimes the simple, yet tedious task of paying your bills can be less anxiety-riddled when you flip the switch or switch emotionally tracks!

"'Enough money' isn't a quantity. 'Enough' isn't out there; it's a relationship to what you already have. Unless you work on that, first (or simultaneously with how you're making money) you will never feel like you have enough, and you will always feel poor. It's possible to feel fat when you're thin, and to feel poor when you're rich. And the thing that changes is your relationship with 'enough.'"

– Geneen Roth

Below are some elements of a sound money self-care ritual:

Check in With Your Body

This fundamental exercise teaches you to notice your physical and emotional responses to money interactions, and Roth encourages her clients to use it any time they confront money in any form. Make it a habit to notice your emotions before you begin any financial task. Be kind to yourself in your thinking – know that feeling overwhelmed with finances is NOT a character flaw, girl. Dealing with finances encompasses a mother-load of mental energy.

I used to think I was lazy and irresponsible for not knowing ALL the details of my budget, my bills, due dates, etc. My heart palpitated every time I logged online to check my balance. I dreaded going to the ATM machine (even when I had money in my account because it represented subtraction; scarcity to me). I avoided the mail and would let it pile up for weeks because I knew it was nothing but bills. Then when it was time to finally check the mail, I couldn't catch my breath and my legs would get heavy, I would send my oldest daughter out to the mailbox instead. But as I evolved on this journey, I came to understand that it really boiled down to a complete lack of awareness about how I felt energetically and emotionally about money.

As you move forward in your journey, you'll notice how your physical and emotional response evolves, too

For example, take out your checkbook, and open your credit card bill or log in to an online account — any financial record you know you'll have to face sooner or later. As you look at the document or website, pause and take a few deep breaths. Observe your physical and mental states with curiosity rather than judgment. Ask yourself if you'd feel better after relaxing or shifting your body a bit. Breathe and summon a sense of compassion for yourself. Be comfortable in the uncomfortable (and trust me, it will feel uncomfortable at first and that is ok.)

Below are some of my favorite money practices to incorporate.

Automate to Focus on Abundance

Anxiety and stress often go together. Worrying about money can lead to stress, which further aggravates anxiety, which contributes to more stressors. It's a vicious cycle. But there are ways to manage one's money—and one's life – to reduce anxiety and increase the overall feeling of satisfaction. One of favorite recommendations is to automate your bills. Again, simple advice, but having your bills come out automatically removes the thought stream of constantly thinking about debt, and ultimately scarcity. And when you do that, you can begin to focus on abundance.

Schedule Regular Money Dates

Each time you sit down and give your money situation your full attention, you have an opportunity to develop helpful skills and infuse your financial life with greater awareness.

Weekly money dates might include paying bills and entering expenses into a bookkeeping system. Monthly dates could entail evaluating how well your spending choices reflect what's important to you, sending in health-insurance claims or purging files you no longer need. There's almost no greater act of self-care than looking out for future you, and future you is going to need some resources. Raises, moves, and new jobs, etc. are all times that you can re-evaluate what you spend and save, and evaluate how much of that you're directing toward short- or long-term needs. And of course, an annual review – the biggest money date of all – involves looking at your accounts and evaluating how they align with your most deeply held values and long-term goals. For example, would you continue to purchase a product if you knew they were violating human rights, or harmful to the environment? Remember, there is power in consciously deciding how and when you decide to spend your money.

Approach money dates as if you're having dinner with an old friend. Bring an open mind, patience, a sense of gratitude and a willingness to forgive. Maybe you'd like to light a candle or have a glass of wine or a beer. You might prefer to pay your bills on a table bathed in natural light. Tessler likes to nibble on dark chocolate and drink tea during her money dates. I personally put on my nicest pjs and start my date after my girls go to bed.

It harkens images of me being a queen starting her important tasks after all of her beloved family and countrymen are well-taken care of. Whatever works for you – just remember to start with a body check-in and maintain a calm awareness as you move through your tasks. Conclude your dates by celebrating the time that you and your money have just spent together. This can be as simple as closing your eyes and thanking money for the opportunity to work with it and telling it that you look forward to working with it again. Voila! You've just asked money out on another date!

Rename Your Expenses

To soften the emotional wallop that often comes with tracking expenses, Tessler proposes using values-based or even amusing names. In place of standard budget-line items such as "Rent" or "Mortgage," she suggests "Sanctuary" or "Love Shack." Instead of guilt-inducing "Vacation Debt," try "Educational Experience Abroad" – and take pride in managing your investment.

Take out a bank or credit card statement (don't forget the body check-in!) and note your major expense categories, listing them by conventional names. Then try some creative renaming. Enter these new names into a bookkeeping program to make them official. Your goal is to make values-based financial decisions less stressful.

Track Your Money

Tracking your money gets me in that fun "game" energy of money. Create a simple spreadsheet where you track all your money that comes in. You don't want to just track your paychecks either. Track when you get gifted money or you get a discount or someone buys you dinner or you find pennies or dimes on the street.

All of this is money you're bringing in. By really giving love and attention to every single penny, you help it to grow. **Where your focus goes, energy flows. If you're focusing on what's coming in, you're going to bring in more money.**

Spend with intention

This is about really taking the time to notice how and why you actually spend your money. Something I like to do is take a deep breath before I actually go to purchase something. Whether it's a piece of clothing, or going to get food, I'll ask myself: what is my intention with spending this money?

Is this showing me that I love myself or is this out of fear? I know that's a funny question, however it really puts things in perspective. I noticed I was purchasing food off of the dollar menu during my lunch breaks (when I already had lunch) when I was stressed out about money and believed this was all I could afford. I was purchasing out of fear and resentment.

Setting financial goals

Having a goal is good for your health. Goal setters and achievers are productive people. Often accomplishes more in one year than a non-goal setter. It's important to set three financial goals: your annual income, savings goals, and retirement goal. It's important to set a goal that is so big, so exhilarating that it excites you and scare you at the same time. Our main purpose in life is to develop ourselves. In order to successfully do this we must always be working towards a goal. What normally trips women up from setting goals is we don't know how to get what we want. So it's the "How" that prevents from setting the goal and moving forward. So we are defeated even before we get started. The goal of a goal is to help us grow. Even if we can't see the entire staircase. Take action with tears in your eyes. Take one step at a time. As you take one step. The next step will be revealed.

Take your time

Have you ever bought something you thought you needed or deserved, and when you look at it you get a pain in your stomach? That feeling is called buyer's remorse. It's time to stop! While you thought you deserved this gadget, you know you can't afford it or aren't looking forward to making payments on it. Before you make your next purchase, take time and decide if the purchase is worth compromising your financial goals and avoid buyer's remorse.

Communicate with your spouse/partner

One of the top reasons couples get divorced is financial stress. Keeping family finances healthy means understanding each person's goals and creating a budget that fits everyone. Take care of your marriage by discussing financial matters with your spouse in a positive and supportive manner.

Keep monthly expenses to a minimum

I know, this is typical, sterile, financial advice, but it is sound. Maintaining a low cost of living means having greater flexibility to meet financial goals like paying off a mortgage or taking a dream vacation. You'll also have less stress because you know your monthly bills are paid **and** that you have an emergency fund to cover expenses should income change. You might even find that you can live on one income and save the other one to help you meet financial and philanthropic goals.

Use cash for everyday purchases

I admit it, budgets suck. But sticking to a budget is more about developing a practice of discipline and getting comfortable with delaying gratification. One of the best ways to keep stress low and stay on budget is to use cash for everyday purchases such as groceries.

Invest for the Future

Taking care of yourself isn't only about spending money on things that help you today. Self-care is also a way to ensure that you're financially secure in the future.

One way to do this is to start investing in a retirement fund. If you have a 401(k) at work, it's a good idea to put the maximum allowable amount into this employer-sponsored retirement plan. In 2019, the max contribution is $18,000 and in 2018, it went up to $18,500. Many employers will also match your contributions dollar-for-dollar, up to 6%. This equals free money for you. To learn more about whether your workplace offers a 401(k) and a match, check with your human resources department.

If your employer doesn't offer a 401(k), you can still set up an IRA on your own. The contribution limit for an IRA is $5,500 in 2017, 2018 and 2019. This doesn't allow you to save as much as you can with a 401(k), but it's still a good way to save for your future.

Save for Emergencies

Sometimes your daily routine is interrupted when the unexpected happens. For example, your car breaks down and you have to pay a large repair bill. Or, you have to go to the hospital, leaving you with a large medical bill – sometimes even after your insurance company has paid up.

The point is you can't predict every expense you'll have. Therefore, you can't budget for all of them. What you can do is start an emergency fund to be prepared to pay for unexpected expenses.

And perhaps, one of the quirkiest, yet most important money self-care rituals:

Be thankful for your bills

I learned this practice from the book "The Magic" by Rhonda Byrne. Every time I get a bill, I write directly on it "thank you for the money." When I pay it I write "paid in full." Every time I get charged on my credit card or receive a bill in the mail, I really think about how lucky I am to be able to pay for a cell phone bill or a heating bill.

We take a lot of this stuff for granted, including having access to clean water or lighting, and access to the Internet. These are things that aren't available everywhere in the world. I take a lot of time to give gratitude to those things and I find doing all these little, tiny practices has made me have a more loving relationship with money and I'm able to bring in more and have fun with the money that does come in.

Remember what I said earlier about Divine design? God is very clear in showing you that you have the power to change your financial situation if you change the way you think about yourself.

CHAPTER FOUR

THE GLOW UP IS REAL

It's your time to step into you who are fully because there's only one you… and the world needs who you're meant to be. Now is the time you really stop playing yourself.

God created you to solve a problem. You are a variable that's missing in someone's equation. Your assignment? Tackle the problem you were uniquely designed to solve on this earth. Now, your assignment may seem small, but it can be the golden link in a great chain of miracles. You are the only You God has anointed for your specific assignment. There is no other You. God created you for progress and increase.

This means you're a reward, not only to yourself, but to someone else. Someone needs you. Somebody wants you. You are necessary to somebody somewhere today. This means that knowing and living in your purpose not only helps you glow it helps others glow as well.

We're all connected. Who you believe you are, how you relate to others and how you engage with the world around you is directly aligned with your purpose. Girl, the glow up is real!

"*Purpose is a soft virtue – but it's what gives you steel in your spine.*"

– Rich Karlgaard

The challenge is that most people never complete their God-given purpose because it takes money to fulfill your purpose in life. Unfortunately, even though money is a tool and vehicle toward fulfillment, it's also a primary barrier that keep us from fulfilling that same purpose. Conversely, there are those who reach a fork in the road where they feel they must choose between earning more money and fulfilling their purpose by doing more good in the world. It doesn't have to be that way.

Knowing and living in your purpose leads to more money. **Money and purpose are not at odds.**

Ladies, it's never a bad thing when science can back up what you feel in your heart and know in your mind. Did you know that a 2016 study published in the *Journal of Research* on personality found that people who felt a sense of purpose accumulated more wealth than those who felt their lives lacked meaning?

The researchers discovered that individuals with a sense of purpose have a higher income and a bigger net worth than those who feel their lives lack meaning.

Even when the scientists controlled for known factors that predict financial success – like demographics and personality – they found a sense of purpose made a big difference in a person's financial life.

PURPOSE... WHERE ART THOU?

Well, the good news is that discovering your purpose and passion in life isn't as difficult as we've been led to believe. It's actually very straight-forward. The magic key to unlocking the earning potential through your purpose is alignment.

"Alignment is the key; there is unlimited power in alignment"
– **Oprah Winfrey**, from her online meditative series
with Deepak Chopra (March 2015)

You and your talent are Divinely Designed. And for every special talent, the world has a unique need that can only be filled by the expression of that talent. Your special mission on this planet is to commit to serve others through your unique creative expression, in whatever form that takes.

Stop obsessing over "finding" your purpose. You're not lost! Once you get out of your head and stop pondering what you're meant to do with your life and instead take action to serve others in any way you can, you'll begin to align with purpose. **It's that simple!** What gets in the way of most people taking action is the courage to go for what they truly want, take chances and be fully seen. **Aligning with your purpose in life requires visibility and vulnerability. It requires pouring your heart into something**

that means the world to you with detachment, and expressing yourself without expectation of outcome. Remember… Fear is a **Liar**!

When I work with my clients on coming into alignment, understanding their purpose and fully embracing their most authentic self, there are five areas I help them explore:

Values and Beliefs. This is a no-brainer and is the foundation of my CTRL-ALT-DEL process introduced in an earlier chapter. In the exercise, I urge my clients (and you) to ask yourself if your values and beliefs still serve you in an authentic way. We tend to not even realize how much our beliefs control us, what we do and what we manifest. This is where we usually have to release old beliefs that don't serve our truth and authenticity, and then begin creating new belief system pathways for our fullest expression of ourselves to come out.

Punching Fear in the Face. AH-ha, yes, now you're beginning to see (hopefully) why I addressed fear so early in the book. It's a biggie. But most people won't initially identify it as fear – they give it watered down names and phrases such as practicality, logic or being realistic because it makes them feel better and safe. And who doesn't want to feel safe, right? But sooner or later, if we're going to walk our authentic path and purpose, we have to answer the question whether change and/or failure frightens you. Fear tends to show our shadow side, where we're keeping ourselves small and limited. Fear is usually attached to our limiting beliefs, so when you rewire your belief systems, your fear begins to dissipate and your power and truth take over.

Listening to your inner voice. We all have intuition for a reason, it too is Divinely designed.

What is your inner voice telling you? Is it pushing you in a direction you haven't yet explored?

Intuition is God speaking to you, your soul's inner guiding light. If you can become more in tune with your body's vibrational compass, it will rarely steer you wrong. Intuition through mindfulness has the power to help you along the path to discovering your authentic self. Learning how to tap in and listen to our intuition helps us discover who we truly are. We tend to be shut off from our own inner guidance system and emotions, so when we begin to learn how to tap back in, incredible things happen and so much fulfillment and abundance can be discovered.

Stop being so Judgemental. Are you hard on yourself, always striving for perfection? Do you compare yourself to others and get discouraged or quit? Judgment is like fear in that it can quickly extinguish your inner light. Comparing yourself to others and harshly judging yourself only slows the process of discovering your authentic self and finding your purpose.

Part of tapping into your authenticity and truth is also learning to see the light and beauty in everything. Noticing you're no different than anyone else brings a sense of community and collective/unity consciousness. This helps us to feel less separate from the universe and thus brings an awesome sense of co-creator power.

Your Energy and Spirituality

Do you feel out of alignment, uneasy, anxious or discontent? Are old spiritual beliefs holding you back from becoming who you're meant to be?

Many Christian women struggle with this because they feel who they are and who they think God wants them to be are in conflict. God would never do that to you! Remember, you're Divinely designed!

When the energy within you and the spiritual beliefs you manifest aren't compatible with who you are, who you're meant to be or who you wish to be, they can put a halt to the growth you must achieve on the path to self-discovery. That's a life-altering consequence.

Understanding your own vibration, energy and life force is a game-changer for developing personal power and truth. When you can go deeper within yourself and begin to feel your own life force, you can begin to understand what's you versus what's not. This helps you create contrast, see your shadow and begin activating your power of choice so you can choose to align with your truth and authenticity over falsehoods.

PURPOSE AND PASSION

I'll let you in on a little secret; for a long time, I didn't fully understand the distinction between passion and purpose. Oftentimes, I would use them interchangeably.

But as I progressed in my career and understanding, the distinction became clear to me. Your passion is what you **love** to do. Your purpose is your mission in life.

It's no wonder the two get mixed up. They're inextricably linked. Passion is the thing that you search for. Purpose was placed inside you from the day you were born. In establishing another key distinction between the two, Ian Gray Simons stated, "Passion is an ego-based emotion and purpose is of spirit."

"Follow your passion, it will lead to your purpose."

Passion alone doesn't provide the greatest fulfillment in our lives. Passion **linked to a purpose** provides the greatest fulfillment in our lives.

Now ladies, allow me to blow your mind (again). When it comes to passion and purpose, it's also important to understand:

You can have multiple passions, but you only have one purpose.

It's possible to have multiple passions because passions are **not** unique to an individual. However, a purpose is unique to every individual, because a purpose takes full advantage of the individual's unique gifts. The purpose I have, to help cultivate a healthy money mindset in Christian women so they chase their dreams, is my own, and it's unique to me.

A passion can be selfish, but a purpose is selfless.

My passions serve no benefit to anybody but myself. I do them for my own pleasure. A purpose, however, involves serving others. As George Krueger and Mary-Lynn Foster wrote, "It's feeling joyful about creating joy. It's about adding value in the lives of others while creating value in your life. It's win-win."

You must find your passion before finding your purpose.

Wait, what? Yes! Think of it like this, "Passion cleans your glasses so that you can clearly see your purpose." My passion for mental and emotional health took me directly to my purpose. Bishop T. D. Jakes remarked, "If you can't figure out your purpose, figure out your passion. For your passion will lead you right into your purpose." **Passion always precedes purpose.**

A passion is best utilized when linked to a purpose.

It was stated earlier that while a passion can be selfish, a purpose is selfless. Indulging in a passion for our own benefit is not a bad thing, but it doesn't give us the sense of meaning that our lives are meant to have. That sense of meaning comes when a passion is linked with a purpose. A purpose gives passion, vision and direction. A purpose keeps the passion going during the inevitable tough times. It's the fuel that keeps the flame going after the initial spark of passion.

Passion and Purpose do not necessarily equate with goals and desires.

Here's another clear distinction, ladies. It is very tempting to confuse your goals and desires with your purpose.

That's because over the course of your life, you'll have a number of desires and goals. They will progress over time based on your experiences, maturity and circumstances. **However, they are not your raison d'etre, your reason for being.**

I'll give you a prime, yet relatable example from one of my clients. She wanted to be a homeowner. For ten years, she rented a very nice home in a nice neighborhood where she raised her children. But the very idea of being the first in her generation to own a home and build a foundation for her family excited her. So, she set a goal to do so. After two years of revamping her credit and saving, she finally purchased her first home. This was a fantastic accomplishment for her!

Now that she has her home, she'll set out to accomplish yet another goal. And then another one. And then another. However, accomplishing these goals, albeit spectacular ones, did not give her a reason to stay alive – purpose does that. And here's where I worked with her on her next level of discovery – helping her uncover her raison d'etre – her reason to get up in the morning, every day of her life.

See, when you discover your purpose, you align with your higher Self, the Self that is Divinely Designed, and you will begin to naturally use all of your mental, emotional and creative energies to develop a skill, talent or interest you love. When that happens, your everyday life takes on new meaning as you share your gift with the world.

For my client, when it came to understanding and nurturing her purpose, she didn't even know where to begin! It was difficult for her to naturally feel or sense her way into knowing what it was, so I worked with her on specific activities to "act" her way into knowing it.

The more we act, the more we get clear on things. I had her participate in activities that acted like experiments to help discover her purpose. These activities included tasks such as volunteering on a non-profit board and chairing their annual fundraiser committee. This was completely new to her, but helped refine and eventually hone in on her passion.

This prescriptive advice can be used by anyone seeking the path of purpose discovery. The only rule is that whatever you are doing in this discovery phase, be sure to do the best you can. Own it. Work it. Give it all that you've got. Do not spend any energy worrying whether or not something will work out, if you should try something, or if you can make money at it, just do it. Remember, this is all about delicious discovery – to see where it leads you. Adopting this perspective will help you get out of your own way and bring clarity through the process of exploring and seeing what works and what doesn't.

PURPOSE, PASSION AND PROFITS?

Your purpose is already within you and it isn't something you look for outside yourself.

It's all too easy to fall victim to siloed thinking that our job, family, passions and desires are all separate and unrelated aspects of our lives. Everything is connected. It's possible to be true to your passions, live a life of purpose and still use business and career as a medium of expression. The result is a life full of abundance.

Yes, girl, you read that correctly: When you follow your passion and live your purpose, abundance follows! Opportunities then begin to present themselves and you find a way to make money while doing what you love!

So how do you find your purpose and make all this possible?

Examine Interest. Interest is paying special attention to some object or thing. It's being definitely concerned about someone or something. Interest is tending to see in the outer world what is already existent in one's mind. Things you think of that give you joy, pleasure, wisdom and satisfaction are interests. What catches your eye? What are you skilled at picking out? Our interests are largely individual because we don't think alike; one person may find interest in some things that another would fail to see. We see in life that which interests us the most and pass blindly by that which is of little or no interest. It's here in this simple practice that many of us may be making our mistakes. We may be so interested in things that are not prosperous, joyful and healthy, that we pass by the very things we desire most and overlook the means of our health and prosperity. With our interest so engrossed in the lesser, either through habit or ignorance, we fail to attract the greater things that are all around us.

Pay Attention. Did you know there is a difference between interest and attention? **Interest is something that piques curiosity. Attention inspires action.** For example, say that you're interested in fashion. You're curious to learn all that you can about the latest styles and how celebrities wear their clothing, Now, take that one step further. All that attention-paying, studying, learning and appreciation, has inspired you to learn fashion design. So, you actually take courses in fashion design. That's the difference between a lover of something and a doer of something; that's the difference between interest and attention.

To have high interest is not enough. We must inject this interest into our daily labors. Our attention must portray our interest, and the keener our interest, the more intense our attention is. Our attention draws facts that are formed in our mind from the outside world. As we direct our attention to our interest, this magnetizes our power of attraction which draws to us much of the same type as our thoughts. When much of our interest is taken up with our full attention, we find that most of our petty and selfish leanings are absorbed by our higher interests and we steadily progress.

All of the steps outlined here can literally transform your life as you start attracting more abundance, earning more and creating financial freedom for yourself.

BREAKOUT AND BREAKTHROUGH… PLOTTING YOUR PATH

Now it's time to inspire a breakthrough. A **breakthrough** is defined as, "a person's first important success." It's the **turning point** where everything shifts for the better! It's these meaningful moments that **change and transform** our lives and the direction we travel. It's the **decision point**. It's the **moment of truth**. A **breakthrough** can be liberating, it can be inspiring, it can be a new beginning for you.

What does a breakthrough look like? Well, it may look different to different women. But the fervent expressing of our desire often looks the same – joy and fulfillment!

I've borrowed an exercise from Barbara Sher's "Wishcraft," called 'Uncovering Your Original Self.' Here's how it works:

Set aside about half an hour for quiet contemplation. (There's no writing involved in this exercise – only thinking.) Let your mind wander back to your childhood. Remember what you used to do to have fun – those times you especially treasured. When you were allowed to daydream or do whatever you wanted, what did you choose to do?

Answer these questions:

- What attracted and fascinated you when you were a kid?
- What sense – smell, sight, hearing, taste, touch – did you live through most? Or did you enjoy them all equally? What kinds of sensory experiences do you remember best?
- What did you love to do (or daydream about), no matter how silly or unimportant it might seem now? Did you have secret aspirations and fantasies that you never told anyone about?

After thirty minutes of unstructured reverie, ask yourself a couple of questions. First, do you feel like there's a part of you that still loves the things you loved as a child? What do you miss most? Next, ask yourself what talents or abilities these childhood dreams and passions might point to in the present. What can you do today to reconnect with some of who you were as a kid?

This is a great first step in helping you uncover your passions and understand your purpose a little better.

PLAYING INTO THE FEAR HELPS YOU PLAY... YOURSELF

Why do we keep talking about fear? I know, I keep mentioning it at every possible turn, but it's so important. Say it with me... Fear is a bitch! Very good.

Understand that fear is there to keep you safe. It creates a nice warm cocoon of predictability, consistency and mediocrity; but we don't look at it that way. No, we rationalize, intellectualize, justify and defend. We don't even acknowledge fear most of the time (unless it's something like spiders or clowns). No, we fake-process our fears and spit out phrases like "play it safe," or "be realistic," or "in a perfect world." But really, these are just the prescriptions your fears give you to keep you in a box.

Safe. Alive. Playing Small. All because you played into your fear.

And when you play small, you play yourself.

I'll give you a prime example. Anyone who knows me knows that I loathe public speaking. Seriously, it's my Kryptonite. Standing (or sitting, my position really doesn't matter) in front of an audience (it could be one person, it could be 10,000, the amount doesn't matter at all), speaking is right up there with drinking boiling poison.

So, of course, I was able to skate through most of my life without having to make any speeches or presentations. But if you think about it, it makes no sense, right? Because in my day job as a therapist, I lead group discussions and staff meetings all the time with no problem. Weird, right?

So fast forward to a time when I decided I wanted to use my gifts and expertise to start my own coaching business. Brilliant, right? I did what most people would do when they're looking to grow and pick up a new skill, I started networking, going to seminars, trainings and conferences. I was immersed in a new world of brilliant minds emboldened with passion and power, and I couldn't wait until I could help others in the same way they helped me.

I started training with one particular coach and loved it. She understood me, understood the work and saw my potential in the field long before I did. I loved watching her interact with us mentees (in small group settings) and the audience (in large conference settings). I loved watching the audiences faces light up with enthusiasm. She captured their attention. She had them hooked. She made it seem so easy.

I wanted to do that too.

So, the time came for me to present to a small group of local women I was coaching as my mentor watched. I knew the topic and I'd been practicing and observing how this process should go for a long time.

I walked to the front of the room. Laptop and all. I cleared my throat. I started to talk, but immediately stumbled with the content. I stumbled over my words. My voice was shaky and low. I fumbled with the laptop. I was sweating. And the sad thing was… I was only in the introduction! The first five minutes!

I couldn't bear going through this any longer. I apologized and got visibly frustrated with the technology (it wasn't the computer's fault) and adjourned the meeting for a 15 minute break. I was so embarrassed. I went into the bathroom and cried. I let my fear play me.

And I played myself.

See, I knew what my fear was. And intellectually, I knew that on the other side of that fear was growth and success. I knew this. But when I got up in front of that audience, I felt myself dying a very slow, painful death. I was overcome with powerful emotions and subsequently negative thoughts, *you're going to look like an idiot. These women are going to talk about you when they get home. Word is going to spread that you're an idiot. You're a fraud. This was so unprofessional of you. Stop this right now so you can save your reputation.* My fear drove my perception of the entire situation. And I gave in.

Fear is so real that it can make you believe your perception is your reality! That's how deep your paradigms of "no" and "you're terrible at this" and "it can't be done" are embedded in your mind. Your comfortable mind, the part that keeps you safe and alive, but playing small will do anything it can think of to keep you away from the "danger" of the unknown. That's why I thought it was okay to postpone an activity right in the middle of doing said activity!

Fear is a liar because it doesn't discriminate. It kills a little something inside its target each and every time. It has one objective only and it doesn't care who you are or where you come from.

So, how did I eventually overcome this process of playing myself? Honestly, by just doing it again. And again. And again. Voice shaking and all, just doing it. And each and every time I proved to myself how brave I am, but more importantly, that I didn't die and no, no one talked badly about me. My reputation was never damaged after these workshops. In fact, it improved!

So that's why we gotta embrace fear. You don't overcome fear by just trying to pretend it's not there. There's no spiritual or emotional growth in ignorance. But there's no growth in avoiding either. You gotta break through that fear. Here are some tips on how to do that.

How to be a wrecking ball on your own Terror Barrier

1. **I ain't never scared. Ok, just kidding, I am but I'm gonna do it anyway.** Bulldoze through it scared. No matter how badly your feet want to stay rooted to the ground. Refuse to permit this negative demon to control you, your emotions and ultimately your future.

2. **Leveling up triggers fear to rear its ugly head.** Every time we attempt to make a major move into an area we've never traveled before, fear wraps around you like a warm blanket. It's as natural as day and night. Where before you used to let it stop you cold, now you simply shrug and

tell yourself, "Oh, there it is again. Well! This must really mean something great for me!"

3. **It's true, on the other side of fear is the glow up.** And the glow is real! It's beautiful. It's the life you've always imagined but thought couldn't be a reality. Think about that feeling. Fall in love with that feeling of accomplishment. Become obsessed with it! I often say if your goal doesn't scare and excite you at the same time, you're going after the wrong goal!

Stop playing yourself. It's okay to be scared, **but do it scared.** Begin to visualize yourself successfully being a wrecking ball on that fear of yours. Mentally see yourself winning. Remember, **perception is reality!**

MAKE YOUR REAL LIFE MOVIE

This is one of my favorite exercises because it's so incredibly powerful. I've used this method for myself, I've used it with some of my patients and with some of the women I've worked with in my coaching business over the years; the results are nothing short of amazing.

Get in a mood, girl! Set aside some real time to be alone. Get some

]magazines, pictures, set some music, light some candles – whatever you need to get in your zone of visualization. The imagination is the most powerful tool we have and I want you to unleash it! Don't hold yourself back at all!

Today, you're going to create a movie that depicts the rest of your life. Yes, you'll be creating your dream life from the ground up. It's like scripting everything that you want for yourself – every detail.

Don't worry about format or grammar. Just be concerned with your desires. One of my favorite coaches, Peggy, uses this method a lot. Below are some of her tips to help you write a script that creates the real life movie of your dreams:

- Handwrite your story in the present tense, as if you are living it **now**. (This helps you energetically let the desires flow from you without editing)
- Create a very positive and uplifting vision of your future. Talk about the things you want **most** in each area of your life – physical body, business or career, finances, relationships, intellect, spiritual connections

- Engage all your senses and include as much detail as possible about where you are, what you look like, who you're with, what you do, your financial situation... everything

- See and feel yourself living in accordance with this script that's custom made for you, by you. The more you feel it, the more real it becomes, and the more powerfully you are attracting it

Once you're done writing, sit for a moment and just meditate on it. Become at ease. Let it process. And then keep it nearby. I wrote mine in a journal that I carry in my purse. I review it every day and I strongly encourage you to do the same. You should read it every day, and refine it as necessary to keep you worked up.

So why is this activity so important (I mean aside from it being a creative activity)? Remember, our imagination is the most powerful tool we have. Our minds are powerful weapons. Therefore, we have to harness the power of visualization:

- Compels you to get very clear on your thoughts about your future. This is one of the most important steps of this process. Getting clear, feeling comfortable and staying clear.

- Helps move you beyond your own limiting beliefs. You're no longer operating from a place of can't or won't.

- Keeps you focused on and attracting what you want rather than what you don't want. No more being stuck in the cycle of compare and contrast.

- Helps unleash your feelings and expectations about your true desires. You've gotta feel the feelings to attract abundance.

- Harnesses the power of the Universe to attract the people, places and resources just as you want them to be. You're getting exactly want you need at the time you need it.

I recommend you take it a step further. Let's make it feel real to become real. In addition to reading it every day, try reading your script out loud (with feeling) and recording it. Then, listen to it several times every day. I suggest listening to it when you wake up and before you go to sleep at night. You can also listen in your car and while you're getting dressed, working out or cooking. Listen to it in the shower. While you're running. Whatever. Just listen to it as much as you possibly can.

With this spaced repetition of new ideas and beliefs, you'll change your thoughts and belief systems (your paradigm). When that happens, your actions will change too.

And the Universe does the rest – opportunities and people who can help will begin to materialize and support you on your journey of becoming the person you want to be and giving you the life you want.

A LETTER TO THE FUTURE

Here's another exercise that's common in self-help manuals. You're going to contemplate and describe the personal legacy you'd like to leave in the world.

Think about how you want to be remembered by your grandchildren or great-grandchildren. In the form of a first-person letter, write a summary of your life, values and accomplishments as you'd like them known to your descendants. Pretend you're near the end of your life and want to share the "greatest hits" version of your personal story for posterity.

Make no mistake: This can be a powerful exercise. Tear-inducing, even. That's okay. By thinking about how you'd like people to remember you after you're gone, you can take steps to align your present self and actions with that ideal vision.

CHAPTER 5

WEALTHY AS YOU WANNA BE

Consciousness is the key to growth. So far, my lovely ladies, we've worked on bringing more awareness into your relationship with money. We've delved into our belief systems surrounding money (which stem as far back as childhood) to our fears and laddered all of that up to our mindset (poverty vs. abundance). You've done a **lot** of work! Please give yourself a round of applause! You are so bomb for going through all of the mucky, ugly, painful and sometimes just plain boring stuff.

Now that you're equipped for battle, it's time to go! But this battle is not in some far off land with an unseen enemy. This is a battle for your hopes and dreams. To move from surviving to thriving. **To be and live as wealthy as you wanna be.**

What's that going to take, Choyo? Well, now that you have the knowledge, it's time to understand and incorporate two very important principles: Knowing your real source of wealth and empowering yourself through action.

THE REAL SOURCE OF YOUR WEALTH

Know that money is not your source of wealth; your connection to God is your source of wealth.

What does that mean? I'll explain it to you from my perspective: it's knowing that when I'm fully locked into a mindset of love and abundance, I feel complete. The seeking for anything melts away when I'm centered within. **If you connect to God (which we can all do regardless of the money in the bank), you'll always feel infinitely wealthy.**

And you do know that God wants you to be wealthy, right? Your being wealthy is a sign of God's blessing in your life, and it's how we're made to live as children of the living king! Your wealth is much bigger than simply having a lot of money. The wealth I'm referring to here is believing in the fullness of God's ability and desire to provide in your life. It's the means – resources, strength and wisdom – to create positive outcomes in the midst of lack. It is light in the darkness, healing in sickness, prosperity in poverty, wholeness in brokenness, favor in obscurity, love for the unlovable, beauty for ashes and victory among victims.

Wealth is a "can do" attitude, a "more than enough" mindset and a "nothing is impossible" belief system. We've already discussed the hallmarks of a wealthy or abundant mindset: it displays itself through radical generosity, extraordinary compassion, sacrificial giving and profound humility. Wealth is always thankful, never jealous, doesn't brag, celebrates others and looks to the future with hope.

We always need to remember that the Lord is the one who gives us the ability and skill to create wealth. When things are going well, it's often easy to take all the credit for the wealth we've accumulated and just as easy to blame God when things go wrong.

- **Thank God daily for any resource you have, big or small.** Thank Him for the water you drink, the food on your plate, the car you drive. Every day thank Him for your job, your salary, your insurance, your clothes, your worn out shoes and your leaky faucet. Through prayerful repetition we start to realize that God is the source for everything we have, which will steadily retrain our mind to see provision and the material world holistically as God sees it.

- **Be a financial blessing.** That includes tithing and giving to charity, for sure, but there may be something more creative and specialized that is suited to your family. Start asking God how to be a blessing with the resources He has given you. Like a faithful employee being trusted to do more substantial work, when you are faithful you may be surprised at how much more He sends your way.

- **Step up your prayer life.** There's no better influence than Jesus, so try to spend as much time with Him as possible. The more we learn to hear His voice, the more we start to see how the world He created really works. God knows exactly how to walk through a difficult situation, financial or otherwise. He also is incredibly creative and has a unique calling just for your family. Wealth for you may or may not look like a 6,000 square foot house or a seven figure trust fund, but God knows exactly what's going to give honor to Him and bring real joy and purpose to your family.

- Ask! The Bible says "you have not because you ask not." If something is on your heart, pray and ask God for it. Maybe that's getting out of debt or getting on track financially. If you really want a promotion, ask for it. If you feel like it's time to change careers, start a side business or take on an exciting new investment, then ask God to give you clarity and to orchestrate that. When we ask, two things are guaranteed to happen. First, God does listen and He is responsive. Second, through conversation He'll start to align your mind towards His brilliant way of thinking. He'll give you creative ideas, new solutions and workarounds. He'll bring helpful connections and turn you away from unhelpful paths. Faith-based finances means being connected with God and that's a pretty incredible thing!

Empower through Inspired Action

You already know by now that thoughts become things. You know you need to focus your thoughts on the things you want, not on the things you don't want. Yet, no matter how well you focus your thoughts on what you want, the Law of Attraction still requires that you take inspired action by acting upon the opportunities that come to you.

To get what you want, you must take inspired action to make your desires reality.

Ideas will come to you, little hunches if you will. They're the kind of thoughts you'll notice, maybe look at, but often dismiss.

Follow these ideas. They're your path to manifesting your desires. If your desire is to be financially wealthy, think of these desires as breadcrumbs that lead you where you want to go.

These breadcrumbs can come in any form, from ideas, to signs on the road, to comments overheard in passing. They are anything that reminds you of what you're asking for.

Often you may ignore them, but they're God telling you to act now to receive what you've asked for. When you follow the breadcrumbs, you're taking inspired action.

Remember, you can't become wealthy if you feel like money is more powerful than you. In order to be in a commanding position with your finances, you have to change your actions with money.

For example, for me, this included creating a savings account (and actually putting money in it), increasing my rates to reflect the worth of my services, being aware of my spending and other steps that helped me feel more empowered with money. My breadcrumb was making small changes that put me in charge of my finances, which increased my confidence, which in turn, strengthened my wealth mindset even more.

The breadcrumbs are God speaking to you. You won't specifically hear, "do x, y and z,'" But God will guide you. He'll show you the way if you'll let Him.

Sometimes you might get these breadcrumbs, but then disregard them because you aren't certain as to their meaning. You need to listen to them. No matter how irrelevant they may seem at the moment, stop, listen and act.

If you want to manifest a car and you have an idea that you should speak to someone or stop by a certain car dealership, those are signs from God. They are inspired actions you're meant to take. If you disregard the idea as irrelevant or come up with reasons why you shouldn't speak to the person or stop at the dealership, you make it harder for you to receive your car.

Similar things will happen if you want to win the lottery. Obviously, you have to take the action of buying a lottery ticket. (You know visualization isn't enough, right?) But you might feel a sudden urge to buy a lottery ticket from a certain store or at a certain time. It could be a place where you've never bought one before. It might even be a nudge that, instead of buying just one, you should buy two. Why? It could be the second one that will be the winning ticket.

The key is to pay attention to your nudges and to act on them.

How do you know if an action is truly inspired?

Sometimes you might feel the nudge to act, but it isn't inspired action. It's coming from your ego, not God.

How do you tell the difference?

Here are some tips:

• Inspired action feels good. Ego-based action is based in fear (fear of losing someone, fear of failure, fear of success…)

- Inspired action is comfortable; it flows. Ego-based action occurs when you feel impatient

- Inspired action is fun. Ego-based action is when you want things to happen in a specific way, such as someone sending you a specific text message after a date.

- Inspired action comes to you unexpectedly. Ego-based action arises when trying to figure out how things will happen.

- Inspired action comes from a place of allowing. Ego-based action is based on attachment to the outcome.

By acting on ideas that naturally and effortlessly flow to you, you'll be guided to increasing your wealth in ways you'd never even imagined were there.

A Little Dose of Reality… Being Rich is a Matter of Mindset… And Habit

Becoming a millionaire may seem like an unattainable dream, but in reality, it's a lot more common than you think. There were 42 million millionaires worldwide in 2018, up from 36 million the year before, according to Credit Suisse's annual Global Wealth Report.

What separates the rich from the poor? You already know mindset plays a huge role. With that mindset comes habit. Let's take some time today to explore the types of habits that foster wealth and success. According to Chelsea Fagan, author of *The Financial Diet*, there are eight dimensions common to millionaires:

- **They don't wait for permission.** From a young age, we're conditioned to get permission to do the things we want. As a result, most of us enter adulthood with the idea that we still need permission to pursue our desires. Wealthy people have shifted their mindset from permission to control.

- **They know the landscape around them.** In the U.S., for instance, we're taught that it's bad manners to talk about money. Most people don't. The wealthy, however, do talk about money – at least among themselves. (From my experience, this is very, very true.) Talking about money helps wealthy people better understand the financial world around them so they're able to make better decisions. Plus, wealthy people actively seek advice and information about money.

- **They ask for help with what they don't know.** This one is huge. From my experience, when poor people don't know something, they tend to shrug their shoulders and go on with life, never seeking an answer. Wealthy people aren't satisfied to remain in ignorance. They have what I call a personal board of directors, a small group of trusted advisors to which they can turn for information and advice. Even if you can't afford to have an accountant, attorney and/or financial advisor, much of the info you need is available for free online. You just have to take the time to search for it.

- **They put a specific (and growing) value on their time.** "Wealthy people decide that every hour of their life has a value," Fagan says, "and they stick to that value while constantly trying to raise it." Wealthy people are aware time is money – and money is time. As a result, they try not to waste time. Fagan urges viewers to treat every hour of their lives as if it has value – because it does.

- **They speak the language of money.** Wealthy people are more financially literate than the poor. They're better educated about personal finance. Because they know what they're talking about, they're better able to advocate for themselves. They're able to make better decisions.

- **They understand that money is a long game.** Or, put another way, **wealthy people recognize that there's no reliable way to get rich quickly, but that almost anyone can get rich slowly**. They keys are persistence and patience. Do the right things for a long time and you will achieve your financial goals. "The choice is not between this $5 Starbucks that will make me happy or this $5 sitting in a sad bank account making me feel bad," Fagan says. "The choice is between this $5 Starbucks today or the hundreds of dollars it has the potential to be when it comes time for retirement."

- **They outsource, outsource, outsource.** Wealthy people are aware of where their skills and talents lie, and they play to those strengths. They know when it's better to delegate a task to somebody who's better at it. And they know when to outsource because their time is better spent elsewhere.

- **They know the importance of recharging.** While you might not have the ability to jet off to a beach house in Florida, we're all able to make time in our lives to "sharpen the saw" as Stephen Covey put it in *The Seven Habits of Highly Effective People*. Don't allow yourself to become overwhelmed. Deliberately dedicate time to self-renewal in your physical life (exercise, proper nutrition), social life (spending time with friends), mental life (reading, education) and spiritual life (meditation, church).

"Money is a result, wealth is a result, health is a result,
illness is a result, your weight is a result.
We live in a world of cause and effect. A lack of money is
never, ever, ever a problem. A lack of money is
merely a symptom of what is going on underneath."
– *The Secrets of the Millionaire Mind* by T. Harv Eker

CREATING AND SUSTAINING YOUR NEW REALITY

We create our own realities, whether we are conscious of it or not (now you are!). Up until now, you were probably unaware of the full power of your thoughts and just reacted to life on auto-pilot, and therefore created your current circumstances unconsciously. This is why it was so important for us to go through all our thoughts and beliefs earlier on it the book – for this very revelation. When you become aware that your thoughts create your reality, you can then consciously choose different thoughts, therefore creating a different reality. This is called "creating consciously." This notion is supported by quantum physics, which suggests that physical reality is created by and differs for every individual.

Yes, girl, you are the creator of our own life! If you don't like what you've created, you can simply choose to change your thoughts to create a new reality for yourself. You're more powerful than you realise!

"All men dream, but not equally.
Those who dream by night in the dusty recesses of their minds,
wake in the day to find that it was a vanity: but the
dreamers of the day are dangerous men, for they may act on
their dreams with open eyes, to make them possible."
– T.E. Lawrence

We are souls on an evolutionary path, here to experience all that life has to offer – whether it be pain or joy. We choose our pains and our sorrows.

What's your dream? Are you living it? Or is it more of a blurry vision, like a mirage teasing you in the distance? The truth is that most people aren't where they want to be simply because they never get started. Perhaps you don't know where to start or perhaps you've been too scared to start. Whatever the reason, just by way of reading this book, you've decided that now is the time to break through the excuses, the fear, the scarcity mindset. You've taken the first step and you're gaining momentum. Once you gain positive momentum, it becomes so much easier to succeed. Here are key principles to harness positive momentum, transform your old reality into one of abundance and sustain it:

- **Surround yourself with positive people.** Limit your exposure to negativity and naysayers by preferring to spend time with folks who have can-do attitudes. Don't listen to the reasons something can't be done; instead find ways to make it happen.

- **Failure happens. Embrace it.** Please know that mistakes are inevitable and should be treated as stepping stones to success rather than signs of weakness or reasons to stop trying. (**This is why it's important not to praise achievement, but to praise effort. The former breeds fear of failure**.)

- **Manage your time effectively.** Recognize that minutes and seconds are a precious non-renewable resource. So, set priorities and pursue them with passion.

- **Ignore the opinions of others.** March to the beat of a different drum – your own drum, girl! Don't feel compelled to "keep up with the Joneses." Limit your exposure to mass media (yes, even social media) not only because it allows you to be more productive, but also because it reduces the influence of advertising and the pressure of cultural norms or fakeness. When investing, don't follow the herd.

- **Have direction.** Act with purpose. Know why you're working hard and saving money. Have a mission, even if it's as simple as putting your kids through college and your daily actions are aligned with your long-term goals.

- **Focus on big wins.** Sure, keep developing smart habits and pay attention to the small stuff. But also understand that if you're diligent with your dollars, then the pennies will take care of themselves. The average person economizes on the small things but isn't willing to make sacrifices when it comes to housing, transportation or career. And the folks who are broke all the time? Well, they fritter away their pennies and their dollars.

- **Do what's difficult.** Don't procrastinate, girl! Practice deferred gratification, sacrificing small comforts today to obtain greater rewards tomorrow.

- **Make your own luck.** Practice awareness so you can recognize opportunities when they come along. Moreover, act boldly, seizing these opportunities where others might hesitate to act.

- **Trust and believe that you're responsible for your own future.** Be proactive. Have a healthy internal locus of control. Understand that although it might not be your fault you're in a given situation, it's your responsibility to change it.

- **Grow and change over time.** Adapt. Evolve. Don't be afraid to entertain different points of view. Most importantly, don't be afraid to change your mind. Seek knowledge and experience, and allow the things you learn to mold you.

THE BLUEPRINT – WEALTH CREATION AND REALITY CREATION

Well, here it is ladies – the Blueprint. The final instruction to staking grace and goodness; financial wealth and abundance in your favor. Brace yourselves. And then Commit. Everyday.

There are so many factors that affect the building or degeneration of wealth. The result of wealth is a combination of all these factors. Some of them we've already gone over in parts. Some of them may be new concepts. But take one of them out and you reduce your ability to create what you want drastically. Most people, when talking about creating wealth, tend to mention only some of the factors and not the rest. That's why it's important to see things in an integrated way rather than in a partial way. Here, I've placed everything in one easy, master list. Please note this master list is a collection of findings from some of the best and brightest thinkers and practitioners in faith, finance, philosophy, health, and personal development. They've provided tried-and-true advice filtered by me. This list has never failed me, nor the clients I work with, therefore I am excited to share it with you!

Tithing and Giving.

Tithing tells God that He is the Source of all that you have in your life. Tithing acknowledges that God is the owner of all things and it's the first and foremost act that opens up the channel of blessings upon you and your world. Giving tells the Universe that you believe you are provided for. Giving is the most direct expression of your belief in abundance. Giving produces physical vibrations of supplication like nothing else can.

Nothing speaks to the Universe louder of your belief in abundance than giving. And when the Universe hears, more will be added unto you. Not as a reward, but because you truly believed in abundance. Giving tells the Universe that you believe you're provided for. Even as you empty your purse, you fear not, demonstrating faith that you'll remain whole, your coffers will be replenished and that your love for whomever you gave, is what's most important. Verily, as you believe these things to be true, you will experience such truths, and abundance will be showered upon you as if the heavens had opened up.

Most times, we think we don't have anything to give. Yet, if we look more closely, we'll see that even the little we have could be shared with others. Let's not wait for a time when we think we'll have lots and then we'll give. By giving and sharing the little we have, we open up the storehouse of the Universe and permit rivers of good to come our way. Take a chance on this Universal principle. Take a chance on yourself. Universal principles always work.

Have you ever experienced a situation where you were asked to donate money to a particular cause, and looking at your shrinking bank balance you were torn between giving money or not? Many people have experienced being in this exact situation, but after deciding to go ahead and make a donation, these same people were very surprised when suddenly a sum of money came to them from some unexpected source to replace the money they just gave away. The truth is, if you hold on to your money, you risk losing the very thing you're hoarding. On the other hand, if you trust good things flow to those who give freely, you'll always have funds available to suit your needs.

When you give, do so freely. Let go of the gift entirely. Recognize the universal scope of the law. Then the gift has a chance to go out and come back multiplied. There's no telling how far the blessing may travel before it comes back. It's a beautiful and encouraging fact that the longer it is in returning, the more hands it's passing through and the more hearts it's blessing. All these hands and hearts add something to it in substance. It's increased all the more when it does return.

Faith and Believing

Faith is positive expectation. Faith is an action. Your imagination is your mental image in action. Faith is also a feeling. Your emotion is energy in motion. Right mental image is right creation. Right feeling is right vibration. Visualizing and feeling are two important components of wealth and reality creation.

The words that you speak. Out of the abundance of the heart mind, the mouth speaks. What you believe in your subconscious mind, you confess with your tongue. Words have power. Where the word of a king is, there is power. Words bring our intentions closer to physical manifestation by turning thought vibration into sound vibration. What the priest says about the value of a thing, so shall its value be. What you appreciate, appreciates in value. What you decree, it shall be unto you.

Whenever you spend money, notice how you feel. If you feel uncomfortable and nervous because you're worried the money might not be replaced, the signal you're sending out is one of lack, and lack will be returned to you. When you spend money, create a positive, peaceful feeling and trust that as you spend you create a vacuum for more money to come into your life. Always stay within your current means of income and at the same time create a vibration of prosperity to create more money coming in the future.

Remember always, that what you are seeking is also seeking you, and whenever you want to sell a particular product of any kind, there is always someone who wants what you have to offer. The buyer may look at many competitors, but yours is the only product he'll buy. Infinite intelligence brings both of you together in divine order.

Joy and Gratitude

To express thanks for something before actually getting it is to mentally accept and receive it into your mental reality. When you mentally receive something, you'll physically receive it. It's said that nature abhors a vacuum. When you give thanks, real, soul-lifting, jubilant thanks for things you don't have yet, nature rushes in to fill that vacuum. It'll fill it with all the things and qualities and people that are bubbling joyously in your heart and mind. Or sometimes it may decide that what you're thankful for doesn't fit you very well, so it'll send you something even better.

God is the joy giver, to give thanks is to express joy back to God for the joy he has given you. The energy you give is the same energy you'll attract. Express joy to God and in return, you gain more joy. Being joyful, contented and happy attracts things that give you such emotions in your life.

Why is it that so many people have a challenge keeping money? Think about it. If you don't treat your significant other with love and respect, do you think that person would want to stay with you? Of course not. Same dynamics apply to money. If you don't treat money with love, respect and appreciation, money wants to leave. It will find ways to avoid you. You'll unconsciously manifest unexpected expenses that will keep you broke, or have just enough to make ends meet.

Start visualizing money coming into your life. When money comes in appreciate it. Don't spend it right away. Give yourself a chance to acknowledge it, look at it and most importantly love it! Pray for money like you'd pray for anything else. Remember, loving money does not mean being attached to it, nor needing it. We are talking about appreciation.

Rejoice in the prosperity of others. When you think negatively of other people acquiring wealth effortlessly, you are thinking the same for yourself. **By being happy for others when money comes to them easily, you're allowing it to come to you the same way.**

Being Prudent and Wise

Business is not charity. Make sure you're getting back for what you give out. Focus all your actions on getting a return for your work. Make sure that you're getting the full value of what you're paying for. In business everyone is there to make money. They aren't in it for charity; don't allow them to make you think that way no matter how generously they try to impress themselves on you. They're only making themselves appear that way so you'll be generous to them. When you let them make you think that way, you'll be subconsciously tricked into responding generously by allowing others to take your money even when you're not fully getting what you want.

In business, it's more profitable to market a good product that is best-selling than the best product that is only good selling. Best-selling products tend to have more energy in motion with collective consciousness. Money is energy that comes to you according to its flow and momentum. Of course, the best combination is the best product that's also best-selling, and which draws in the most sales on a consistent basis. It's always wise to go for products that are more saleable than those that are not.

Always follow: Be sharp, shrewd and subtle. This is the true meaning of being sharp and shrewd as a business person. When you give outside of business, give freely. But when you give in business, give business-mindedly. In the world of business, you have to mean business. This is prudence.

Growing and Contributing More Value

Your income will grow only to the extent that you do. Your outer wealth is meant to be a reflection and manifestation of your inner wealth. Your outer wealth is the measure of value that you have given to the world. Strive not to be a woman of success, but rather strive to be a woman of value.

You can only give if you first receive. Gain wisdom and awareness. How can you handle power unless you have the wisdom for it? The Universe can't provide you with more unless you've shown some degree of maturity by simply managing whatever amount you already have. Energy is managed according to God's subconscious law of waste not, want not.

When you gain wisdom and awareness, you gain the ability to handle power. Money is power. All wealth is the offspring of power, possessions are of value only as they confer power. Events are significant only as they affect power. All things represent certain forms and degrees of power. Money is a manifestation of power.

People are making so much money not because they're smarter than you, and not because they're more disciplined. Most of the time, they just stumble onto a few tricks and those tricks are enough to put them on the winning side of the curve. Life is not fair, and a few advantages, often formed from random experimentation are enough to separate the winners from the rest. The gulf between the two is absolutely massive. One moment you're broke, the next you're wealthy. There's no middle ground. Knowledge is power. All you need is the right information in your hands and you can use it to make yourself rich beyond your wildest dreams.

Intention, Goal, Money Consciousness

Intention is focus. What you focus on expands. You attract everything and anything you hold in your mind whether wanted or unwanted. Focus on money and that is what you will manifest. To be wealthy requires one to have a money consciousness. Desire force is the attracting power that pulls what you want to you and pulls you to what you want.

Try to imagine a lot of money in your mind. Does it look clear or fuzzy? Now try to imagine a crisp $100 bill in your mind. Is that image clear or fuzzy? It needs to be clear for you to manifest it. That's why having clear, well-defined and specific goals is so important. Don't worry about not wanting to limit your ability to achieve by setting numbers to your goal. The aim is to make it easy to manifest first. You can always keep increasing the limits and expand the boundaries of your goal as you move nearer to it. This is the real meaning of practicality.

Being open to opportunity and seizing the moment.

Go with the mindset of expecting opportunity and being ready to seize it when it appears. You won't find it as often as you could if you're not on the lookout for it, and you can't capture it unless you have the mind for it. You create opportunities in reality according to your positive expectations. Focus on putting yourself in as many situations and circumstances where good luck can occur as possible. Then you'll get your share.

Slow is harder than faster, because it's almost impossible to create momentum while moving slowly. Rather than waiting for people to discover and engage you, choose to take proactive action in creating what you want. Successful people are highly proactive people because they are a dominant force in reality. Dominance is attractive and is shown by taking initiative rather than being passive. Of course, there should be a balance in deciding when you wait for others to discover you and when you choose to tell them about you instead.

Marketing and Testing

The two most important skills required for success in business are expert knowledge in your field and marketing. The first thing is to have something of great value to give, the second is to communicate this offer to as many of the right people as possible in the best ways possible. Marketing is all about communicating your value to the world.

Be open to all possibilities. Be willing to try new ideas. You never know what you can achieve until you try. Testing is one of the greatest ways to produce enormous amounts of results with the smallest actions. One little change can cause a big difference in the performance of the whole system. Testing helps you to get the most results from something.

The secret of succeeding very quickly is to quit like crazy. Quit what you feel isn't working for you, or what you find isn't what you want or like. Don't be a fool persisting in what you don't believe really suits you. Quit faster, give up. Keep trying new things and testing. Persist only in that which you believe you can make work for you. From one perspective, Edison was a super quitter. He quit ten thousand times rapidly until he finally found success. Look for what's easiest to do, that can take you in the direction you want to go. In this mentality there's no quitting, there's only testing. So, reframing the Edison example makes him a super tester. He tested the hell out of everything until he found what worked. Test as short as possible to get the necessary data you need and then make the next test.

You can quite happily spend time trying out new things only to see them flop. All it takes is one success, and you can enjoy all the rewards it brings you. Be prepared to try three things; two may be flops but one is the success you're looking for.

Breaking mental limits and rules of doing

All limits are mental. The only thing stopping you is the mind. The only thing that can free you is the mind. You are the mind. You are the one restricting or liberating yourself. All obstacles are mental blocks. Remember, there are no rules, there are no limits. When you can remove the limits of a thing in your mind, anything is possible for you and you can do it more powerfully than anyone else. Allow blessings to come from any place and anyone. Be open to money in whatever form flowing into your life by feeling you're worth the money or it's worth getting money.

Placing preconceived expectations on how your intention should manifest may unnecessarily limit your results. For example, if you believe an action plan is necessary and you filter your intention through that belief, then you're limiting yourself to manifesting your intention through a smaller field of possibilities (those that involve the creation of an action plan). You may miss out on some wonderful opportunities to manifest money in ways that involve no plan whatsoever.

Whatever is truly necessary for you to manifest an intention will come to you as part of the manifestation itself. If knowledge is necessary for you, you'll manifest that knowledge. If an action plan is needed, that plan will come to you. If better circumstances or opportunities are required, your circumstances will change. For each person who thinks a certain criteria is necessary to manifest a certain goal, you can probably find someone who did it without that criteria. People have attained that particular goal in a variety of different ways.

Don't restrict the way your intention manifests unless you have very good reason. Remain open. Accept all possible pathways for your desire to enter your life. Simply hold the intention, and let it play out however it wants. God is unlimited, we limit God. Sometimes it's better not to think about the possibilities so you don't reject them. When they arise in the moment, flow with them.

Break all the rules in order to win. All good work is done in defiance of management. It's a shame that smart people at every sizable corporation have to lie, cheat and connive to circumvent dumb policies every day. Whatever the majority of people is doing, under any given circumstance, if you do the exact opposite, you'll probably never make another mistake as long as you live. Do what you want and do it your way.

Creating Subconscious Impressions of Wealth.

By choosing to buy the best and quality products for yourself, you are saying you're worth it, that you're the best. Your subconscious mind will pick up these impressions from your actions and create conditions in your life that resonate with that state of mind.

When you keep a good amount of cash in your wallet and leave money lying around in your home where you can see it, your subconscious mind will be constantly impressed with the idea of supply and abundance. By causing yourself to feel abundance, you'll perpetuate the conditions of abundance in your life.

The subconscious impression of abundance creates conditions of abundance. Seeing abundance in one area creates a mental shift and allows you to start seeing and feeling more abundance in every area of your life. The key is to get more conscious references of abundance so you can impress upon your subconscious mind as much as possible the reality of abundance.

Trusting God, detachment and letting go

Let go and let God. Anything you want can be acquired through detachment, because detachment is based on resting in the complete grace of God and knowing that He's always working through you for your greatest good.

To be detached is to realize that everything good is from God and nothing at all is from you. God is working through you and the other elements in your reality, so there's nothing to hold onto as your own.

All you have to do is to hold the right beliefs and let God do the work. When you're detached, your desires manifest much faster.

Wealth is more than money. It's also happiness, self-esteem, freedom, health and love. You can focus on increasing any of these areas to increase your overall condition of wealth.

CHAPTER SIX

BYE BYE MONEY TRAUMA DRAMA

Whew...we made it! Well, you made it. Believe me when I say that I am so incredibly grateful that you even considered picking up my book and trusted me enough to read it AND participate in the activities. I know that sometimes, my words and my directions may have come across as trivial. "What is this lady talking about?" Or perhaps "easier said than done," was a thought. And you probably felt uncomfortable. A LOT.

And that's okay. That's when you know you're onto something BIG.

See, I hate the saying "change is hard." It doesn't highlight the real resistance which is "learning new ways to respond to and behave with change is hard." I believe that every human being welcomes positive change in their lives. They want more money, more freedom, more peace, more joy, more ice cream...whatever... but the process that comes with influencing that change is a new way of thinking and being. THAT's the hard part. You've already learned and adapted modes and programming that serve the old ways...it takes a hell of a lot of undoing, relearning, reprogramming and redoing to ingrain NEW modes. Yes, it's hard.

So, what happens is we want more money. We want to live to our fullest, God-given, Divinely designed talent and purpose, but our Ego and our programming FREAKS OUT! "Danger Will Robinson!" After all, our Ego and programming were custom built to keep us safe. For example, "Don't try that, you're crazy to think you can make a million bucks. Only people who go to an Ivy League school can do that. They make the right connections and get access to the right resources. You don't have any of that. Just keep working at your job and be happy for what you have. At least you have a job and can put food on the table."

In this example, your Ego is telling you that playing it safe and small will keep you from being disappointed and destitute. Your programming has a handshake agreement with your Ego and is telling you that a million dollars is an insane amount of money for you to strive for because you're not part of an elite set of individuals, so don't bother. Both Ego and programming embrace fear and lie to you. And KEEP. YOU. HERE.

I know. It's a battle I fight every day. Now, please believe me when I say it gets easier over time. It's like getting in the ring with the same boxer over and over again. For the first 70 rounds, you get the snot beat out of you. And you can't understand why. You're in the best shape of your life – you trained hard and you beat every other boxer you went up against up until this point. You're using all of your best moves. **And they keep beating you.**

Dejected, you're thinking about giving up the goal of beating this boxer. It's pointless. You have to be super human to best this person. And you're not. You convince yourself as a consolation, you'll stay involved in the industry – just as a referee instead.

But your coach (that's me) says to you "Hey, it's not because they are better than you physically, they are beating you mentally. I know it feels like a lot of pointless work, but we're going to sit down and watch all of the replays of your fights. I'm sure we'll learn something that will be useful in your next match."

But you're thinking "Seriously? There's nothing that you can show me that I haven't already experienced in defeat." But, because you're a fighter (in more ways than one), you reluctantly take my advice.

And what do you know? You notice patterns… your opponent pretty much sticks to the same moves. Just at slightly different times. And you notice your patterns… every time your opponent throws a punch, you pull out your fastest, hardest punch or new move. But it doesn't work. And then you get tired. Funny how you've never noticed it before. All this time, you're trying your hardest and FAILING and your opponent was being basic and predictable the whole time. Girl, don't you feel silly?

But you shouldn't. Now that you know their moves, you're ready to get back into the ring. And you begin to win. Your confidence starts to increase. You begin to gain more clout. Your purse (money) increases because you're on a winning streak. – You're leveling up.

This newfound prestige is all so new to you that it's kind of exciting but scary.

And now the same opponent wants a rematch. But you think you've got the strategy down pat – so you accept the challenge.

Much to your surprise you lose the first 3 rounds. What? But instead of giving up, you call a timeout (do those even exist in boxing, IDK, I'm just gonna go with that because it works for my parable :)). You confer with your Coach and analyze all your opponent's moves as well as yours. Again, you see patterns. On both sides. That tricky opponent learned something, but you're smarter. You learned more. Now you know what you need to do.

You go back into the ring. And voila! You win. And you keep winning!

Your opponent retreats. For a while. But even when they come back, you'll be prepared. Because now you're not afraid to lose. You know that by losing, you learn invaluable information that helps you become a better boxer. You're are no longer shadowboxing, you know the patterns. And you'll keep winning.

The same is true for your money. When you know the patterns, you can dismantle the ones that no longer serve you. And of course, relearn or reinforce that ones that support your goal. When you know your patterns, you're no longer shadowboxing with life.

But you're gonna have to do a whole lot of failing first. There are so many small wins in those failings because it gives you insight into what's not working. You've gotta be willing to understand, acknowledge and accept as Truth that God has given you the beautiful gift of Free Will and Control. And because you have those gifts, do not squander them. Understand that He has given you power to create your life. He loves us that much.

But you've got to be willing to do the work. Know the patterns, know the programming, and then you change; change and create new and better behaviors.

Remember earlier I said that I battle with my programming every day? Yes, I literally wake up, and I pray and acknowledge to God that whatever obstacle I am presented with that day, that I will rely on my strength, courage and wisdom to recall that I am Divinely designed and uniquely qualified to overcome. That I will press my way through my internal fears, lies and weaknesses to receive what I deserve.

The human experience will compel you to actively and consistently practice gratitude, compassion and intentionally affirm your power and Faith. And that's a beautiful thing. Even when it's a real struggle.

There will always be struggle. Living a life that is replete of money does NOT negate all of the negative things we all encounter – betrayal, disappointment, rejection, abandonment, etc. But we are all a living testament to His Love. And I know that when we learn to control our thoughts, feelings and behaviors in response to the beautiful ups and downs in life, we drastically evolve and improve our relationships with all things material and spiritual.

My journey is filled with promise. I am more proud and excited to call myself a Christian than ever before. It's no longer a title or a category. Now it's a bountiful and dynamic relationship with God and the world. I see myself as powerful and understand my purpose.

Over the years, my relationship with my family and loved ones has been tested – all being in various forms of disarray. But it wasn't until I was able to bravely go inside myself and touch and heal my soft spots that I was able to heal and rebuild the soft spots in my life.

Remember, As above, so below. As within, so without.

Pain is a gift. Trauma can be healed. And I hope you've come to recognize that a lot of our money traumas (our blocks) are directly related to emotional traumas that we've endured but never healed in life.

Your purpose is definitely NOT to live with money trauma. No more money trauma drama. By picking up this book, you literally proclaimed to the Universe "This stops now!"

Baby, you're on your way.

I'm still on this journey. I've been broke. I've been rich. Then broke again. But after healed and hustled, I am rich on purpose.

You can be, too.

ABOUT THE AUTHOR

Choyo Wilson-Daniel, LPC, is one of their premiere Mindset Coaches for Christian women. She founded Loveshift Coaching in 2018 to support women who long to run their own business, on their own terms, so that they can make a powerful difference in the world.

A seasoned entrepreneur, Choyo recalls her own struggles as a business owner, "I longed to be an entrepreneur who made an impact. But every time I'd try to move forward, I felt blocked. I'd go full force toward a new business idea, and then – as quickly as it began – it would fizzle out." The breakthrough came when she started loving, appreciating, and being herself.

Now, she has supported and empowered hundreds of women by showing them how to be a richer person inside and out while still maintaining their connections to God, their husband and children. "My most important work is helping women stay true to their own purpose so that they can create limitless prosperity."

A licensed clinical therapist by trade, and author, Choyo travels around the country speaking to women and girls about nurturing a healthy money mindset. She resides in Guilderland, NY with her husband Charles and daughters Hannah and Olivia.

Money Mindset Coaching

In all of my years of working as a Therapist and Mindset coach, I found that there is a special group of women in the land of money roadblocks. They are successful women. Business owners, influencers and professionals. Maybe the only one who had made it in their family. They can't enjoy the money they have because of their constant fear of losing it.

Their success is limited by the financial glass ceiling they've created in their mind. Their comfort zone has them doing OK when they could do AMAZING.

Behind the designer stilettos and the expensive lace front wigs, they feel unworthy and guilty for having money.

That's why I set out on a mission to find out why so many women struggle with their finances and are living paycheck to paycheck even though they have a business or a good job with benefits.

I'VE HELPED HUNDREDS OF AMAZING WOMEN OF GOD, JUST LIKE YOU, IDENTIFY AND UNPLUG THE MONEY BLOCKS THAT STOP AN INFINITE FLOW OF MONEY TO THEIR LIVES.

That's why I set out on a mission to help women who struggling with their finances and are living paycheck to paycheck even though they have a business or a good job with benefits.

As your Money Mindset Coach, I help you identify your money blocks and improve your overall relationship with money:

- Money Paradigm Mastery: How to identify and change your natural habitual thinking of money into a prosperity consciousness that seeps into your subconscious so you can live a more prosperous life.

- Wealth Map: You'll become crystal clear on what you want in life.

- The Money Paradigm: The fastest and simplest way to change the way you view your finances. How to upgrade your mental programming to keep it operating at optimum level.

- Money Blocks Uncovered: How to expose your mental money block and retrain your brain to overcome any mental or emotional hurdle in your relationship with money so you can shatter your financial glass ceiling.

- The Courage To Ask For Your Worth: The truth about how childhood affects how you PRICE your products and services or negotiate your salary TODAY... and will affect your long-term success twenty years from now. Get this wrong and you will forever be stuck in Entrepreneurial Poverty.

- Universal wealth strategy: Why money doesn't equal wealth and what actually does so you can secure true prosperity for your family for generations to come.

- Money Story Retold: How to craft your new money story where there is always a financial happy ending.

- Money Relationship Therapy: How to reinvent your relationship with money so it's not based on guilt, shame or anxiety.

- The Successful 1% Psychology: How to think like the 1% and earn like the 1%

- How to blast self-doubt out of the water and overcome fear: This life changing strategy will guarantee lasting results in anything you do.

For more than 15 years, I have helped countless women conquer their inner game and revamp their relationship with money. My Signature Coaching Program are designed to support whatever your money life goals are – whether it is to increase revenues from tens of thousands of dollars into the millions for your business, birth a new brand, or reposition yourself as a leader in your industry to secure that promotion, working with me will help you create the life you always wanted.

BOOK YOUR FREE 30-MINUTE DISCOVER CALL TODAY AT: HTTPS://CHOYODANIEL.AS.ME/

www.ingramcontent.com/pod-product-compliance
Lightning Source LLC
Chambersburg PA
CBHW050553210326
41521CB00008B/949